ANGELS *AND* SAINTS

"This well-sourced book facilitates a deep understanding of angels and saints with crucial sensitivity to our individual approaches to prayer, Mass, love, and God. Elizabeth Klein has created a brilliant reflection that reminds each of us how and why we are all members of the Communion of Saints."

Jane M. Spanich
Theology department, St. Thomas Aquinas High School
Fort Lauderdale, Florida

"It's heartbreaking that so many people plow through the desert of life blind to the heavenly friends and refreshments available to us. Elizabeth Klein's smart, concise, and engaging treatment of the angels and saints in Catholic tradition unveils who these wonderful, holy helpers are and how they stand ready to help us."

Tanner Kalina
Cofounder of the *Saints Alive* podcast

"We are never alone, never without help. Our society is as large as heaven and Earth combined, and we're created to be on friendly terms with its heavenly inhabitants. This is reality as God has revealed it to us, and Elizabeth Klein has made unforgettably immediate in her book. It will change the way you pray and the way you go about your days."

Mike Aquilina
Author of *Angels of God*

ENGAGING CATHOLICISM

ANGELS AND SAINTS

Who They Are and Why They Matter

Elizabeth Klein

McGrath Institute for Church Life | University of Notre Dame

Ave Maria Press Notre Dame, Indiana

Nihil Obstat: Reverend Monsignor Michael Heintz, PhD
Censor Librorum

Imprimatur: Most Reverend Kevin C. Rhoades
Bishop of Fort Wayne–South Bend
Given at Fort Wayne, Indiana, on May 18, 2023

Founded in 1865, Ave Maria Press is a ministry of the United States Province of Holy Cross.

www.avemariapress.com

Paperback: ISBN-13 978-1-64680-237-1

E-book: ISBN-13 978-1-64680-238-8

Cover image "Five dancing angels" by Giovanni di Paolo (1403–1482).

Cover and text design by Samantha Watson.

Printed and bound in the United States of America.

Library of Congress Cataloging-in-Publication Data is available.

CONTENTS

Part II: Saints

ABOUT THE ENGAGING CATHOLICISM SERIES

Doctrine is probably not the first thing that comes to mind when we consider the pastoral work of the Church. We tend to presume that doctrine is abstract, of interest primarily to theologians and clergy whose vocation it is to contemplate lofty questions of belief. On the other hand, we tend to think the pastoral life of the Church is consumed primarily with practical questions: How do we pray? How do we pass on faith to the next generation? How do we form Christians to care about the hungry and thirsty? How might our parishes become spaces of lived discipleship? What are the best practices for the formation of Catholic families? Presenting at catechetical conferences in dioceses on a specific point of Catholic theology, faculty and staff of the McGrath Institute for Church Life often hear the question, "So, what's the significance? Give me the practical takeaways."

The separation between doctrine and practice is bad for theologians, pastoral leaders, and Christians looking to grow in holiness. It leads to theologians who no longer see their vocation as connected to the Church. Academic theologians speak a language that the enlightened alone possess. On occasion, they turn their attention to the ordinary beliefs and practices of the faithful, sometimes reacting with amusement or horror that one could be so primitive as to adore the Eucharist or leave flowers before Our Lady of Guadalupe. The proper arena for the theologian to exercise her craft is assumed to be the doctoral seminar, not the parish or the Catholic secondary school.

Likewise, pastoral strategy too often develops apart from the intellectual treasury of the Church. Such strategy is unreflective, not able to critically examine its own assumptions. For example, how we prepare adolescents for Confirmation is a theological and pastoral problem. Without the wisdom of sacramental doctrine, responding to this pastoral need becomes a matter of pragmatic conjecture, unfortunately leading to the variety of both implicit and often impoverished theologies of Confirmation that arose in the twentieth century. Pastoral strategy divorced from the doctrinal richness of the Church can leave catechesis deprived of anything worthwhile to pass on. If one is to be a youth minister, it is not enough to know best practices for accompanying teens through adolescence, since one can accompany someone even off a cliff. Pastoral leaders must also know a good deal about what Catholicism teaches to lead members of Christ's Body to the fullness of human happiness.

The Engaging Catholicism series invites you to see the intrinsic and intimate connection between doctrine and the pastoral life of the Church. Doctrines, after all, are the normative way of handing on the mysteries of our faith. Doctrines make us able to pick up a mystery, carry it around, and hand it to someone else. Doctrines, studied and understood, allow us to know we *are* handing on *this* mystery and not some substitute.

In order to properly hand on the mysteries of our faith, the pastoral leader has to *know a given doctrine contains a mystery*—has to have the doctrine opened up so that receiving it means encountering the mystery it carries. Only then can one be transformed by the doctrine. The problem with religious practice unformed or inadequately formed by doctrine is that it expects an easy and mostly continuous spiritual high, which cannot be sustained if one has sufficient grasp of one's own humanity.

We in the McGrath Institute for Church Life have confidence in Christian doctrines as saving truths, bearing mystery from the God who is love. We believe in the importance of these teachings for making us ever more human, and we believe in the urgent need to speak the Church's doctrines into, for, and with those who tend the pastoral life of the Church. We cannot think of any task more important than this. The books of this series represent our best efforts toward this crucial effort.

John C. Cavadini
Director of the McGrath Institute for Church Life
University of Notre Dame

FOREWORD

After two decades of teaching the Bible in various college, seminary, and church settings, one thing I continue to notice is that *everyone* is fascinated by angels. Whether my students are believers or unbelievers, young or old, learned or not, whenever the topic arises of the spiritual creatures that scripture refers to as "angels" or "messengers" (Greek *angeloi*), I am usually hit with a barrage of questions, such as:

- Do angels really exist?
- Are guardian angels real?
- What about the fallen angels, commonly known as "demons"?
- Do human beings become angels when we die?

And so on and so forth. Clearly, when it comes to the angels, many people have lots of important but often unanswered questions.

By contrast, when it comes to the men and women commonly known as "saints," the situation is quite different. In my experience, many people seem to be fairly certain that they know what a saint is—someone who has been "canonized" by the Church for living an extremely holy life and who is now in heaven. In other words, a "saint" is something a person becomes *after* they die. This view is often coupled with an idea of sainthood as a virtually unachievable state, a spiritual goal that can only be reached by the very select few. Students are often very surprised when I point out to them that in the New Testament, the word "saint" or "holy one" (Greek *hagios*) is actually used for *believers on earth*. For example, the apostle Paul addresses one of his letters to "the saints who are in Ephesus and are faithful in Christ Jesus" (Ephesians 1:1).

In her wonderfully accessible book, Dr. Elizabeth Klein draws on her scholarly expertise in angelology (the theology of angels) as well as her extensive knowledge of Church teaching and the writings of church fathers to shed light on the many unanswered questions and misconceptions that often swirl around the mysterious figures of the angels and the saints. She takes the reader, step by step, on a guided tour of exactly what sacred scripture and sacred tradition—as opposed to often wild and unfounded speculations—reveal to us about them. The result is a wonderful study that sheds fresh light on the mystery of our communion with the beings who sing the eternal song recorded in the pages of the Apocalypse: "Holy, holy, holy, the Lord God the Almighty, who was and is and is to come" (Revelation 4:8).

As Dr. Klein shows, far from being either unreal or unimportant, the angels and saints are the invisible guardians and spiritual companions of those of us who are in Christ but still on earth and still growing in holiness as we journey toward the heavenly promised land. This beautiful book shows exactly who the angels and saints are and why they should play a key role in the spiritual life of every Christian.

Brant Pitre
Distinguished Research Professor of Scripture
Augustine Institute

INTRODUCTION

And so, with all the angels and saints,
we praise you, as without end we acclaim:
Holy, Holy, Holy . . .

These words, taken from the Eucharistic prayer said in the Mass, paint a beautiful picture. They tell us that although our experience of the Mass is often humdrum, we are in fact being swept up into the liturgy of heaven, where the angels and saints praise God before his throne, face-to-face. By joining in their song, we are supposed to get a glimpse of eternity—and perhaps, on occasion, we actually sense something of that kind during Mass. But who are these legions of invisible worshippers whom we are said to join in eternal praise? Our vision of the heavenly liturgy can be a bit blurry—or at the very least, much less magnificent—if we have little understanding of the company that we are in, and what a company it is!

This book will help to bring your vision into clearer focus and to give more definition and shape to that mysterious cloud of witnesses (see Hebrews 12:1). Because, despite the fact that angels and saints are the subject of many popular devotions, a number of misconceptions surround them.

As for the angels, they have been appropriated by just about everyone, whether religious or not. Their images can be found in backyard gardens and on children's clothing nearly as often as they can be found in great cathedrals. Most misconceptions about angels fall into one of two categories: over sentimentalization or abstraction. The sentimental angels are seen as fair-haired youths whose only job is to look beautiful, play the harp, and occasionally protect children. On the other extreme, the angels are seen as an abstract theological category, so obscure that only the most learned theologians would bother to think about them at all. The scholastic theologians, after all, were accused by the Protestant Reformers of being utterly pedantic because they supposedly asked questions such as how many angels can dance on the head of a pin. But neither of these caricatures accurately represents what the Church believes to be true about angels. Angels are creatures made by God, just like human beings, and they are every bit as individual as we are. They respond to God in love and do his will. How and why they do this we shall see in the course of this book.

As for the saints, they likewise fall prey to the fancies of our weak imaginations. The cult of the saints was criticized heavily during the Protestant Reformation as manifesting the worst of Catholic superstition. The saints can sometimes appear to outsiders as the Catholic version of demigods, and their veneration understood as the outpouring of a kind of pagan impulse for hero worship. At best, such practices are left to the unlearned masses; at worst, they are idolatrous distractions from the worship of God. But for Catholics, saints populate our religious imagination. We name our churches and children after them, and we look to them for help. This book explores our Catholic practices and shows why the Church not only tolerates these devotions but encourages them. The saints are not demigods, nor are they in competition with God; they are human beings like ourselves who have died in friendship with the Lord and now live with him in heaven. They are our friends and fellow members of the Body of Christ who simply happen to have died.

As the words of the liturgy cited above suggest, the Church's teaching about saints and angels is a beautiful thing, one worth learning not simply so that we can defend it when speaking to non-Catholics (although that is, of course, useful), but also so that we can approach the Mass, our private prayers, and the Church's liturgical calendar with better understanding, and therefore also attend to them with more fervent love. I hope this book will help facilitate this growth in understanding and love, as you come to see what the Church has to teach us about the angels and saints of God.

PART I
ANGELS

1.

WHAT DOES THE BIBLE SAY ABOUT ANGELS?

The topic of this chapter is ambitious, because angels feature in many biblical stories, and some of the most important and famous stories at that! To name but a few examples from the Old Testament: angels visit Abraham under the oaks of Mamre (Gn 18:1), an angel prevents Abraham from sacrificing his son Isaac (Gn 22:11), and an angel is said to speak from the burning bush (Ex 3:2). In the New Testament, an angel announces the birth of Christ to the Virgin Mary (Lk 1:28), an angel tells Joseph to take Mary as his wife (Mt 1:20), and an angel announces the Resurrection of Christ (e.g., Lk 24:6–7). The ubiquity of angels in the Bible leads St. Augustine to tell his congregation in a homily: "We know from our faith that angels exist, and we read of their having appeared to many people. We hold this firmly, and it would be wrong for us to doubt it" (*en. Ps.* 103.1.15; trans. Maria Boulding). So the presence of angels throughout the biblical text teaches us, at the very least, that they exist and that their existence is part of the deposit of faith.

Nevertheless, despite the angels playing a part (one might even say a leading part) in the drama of salvation history, the Bible tells us little about their origin or their nature. Although direct information about the angels is particularly limited, this kind of silence is actually quite typical of the biblical text. The Bible tells us about humankind through stories, and likewise God is revealed primarily through his interactions with the people of Israel and rarely through direct theological explanations. So it should come as no surprise that if we want to contemplate the angels, we must meditate on the stories of the Bible to come to a deeper understanding of who they are. Let's take a closer look at three of the stories we have already mentioned: the visitation of the angels to Abraham, Moses and the burning bush, and the Nativity of Christ.

At the beginning of Genesis 18, we are told that "the LORD appeared to Abraham by the oaks of Mamre, as he sat at the entrance of his tent in the heat of the day" (Gn 18:1). This visitation of the Lord, however, is not like the visitation of the glory of the Lord to the prophets—such as Ezekiel's vision of the wheel chariot (cf. Ez 1). Nor is it the kind of presence like that of the Lord in the tabernacle or the Temple, which is often accompanied by a cloud or fire (see, for example, Numbers 9:15). Rather, Abraham "looked up and saw three men standing near him. When he saw them, he ran from the tent entrance to meet them, and bowed down to the ground" (Gn 18:2). Abraham proceeds to wash the men's feet and to offer them cakes of flour and a tender calf with curds and milk. After the meal, the purpose of the men's visit is revealed: to announce to Sarah and Abraham that they will have a child in their old age. When the men depart from Abraham's camp, they disclose that they are headed to Sodom and Gomorrah to pronounce judgment on that city. However, in the passages discussing the judgment of these wicked cities, the story once again only refers to the Lord speaking, although all three men are still on the scene. It is not until the beginning of Genesis 19 that we are told explicitly that it is not mere men but two *angels* who continue on their way to Sodom.

When we read this story in order to discern the relationship of God with angels (and angels with humans), it is extremely confusing! Many of the church fathers puzzled about this passage, wondering if we are to understand only one of the three men as God (the one who does not go on to Sodom) and the other two men as angels. But, as St. Augustine points out, Abraham addresses all three of the angels in the singular as Lord and falls down before all of them to pay homage. The three likewise appear to answer him in unison. Are we then to understand these three men as some kind of image or appearance of the Trinity—that is, that the Father, Son, and Holy Spirit all appeared to Abraham? If so, why do only two of them continue on to Sodom? The difficulties seem hopeless to disentangle. But let us leave these questions about Genesis 18 and 19 for a moment and collect some more data points.

Let us add to our considerations the story of the burning bush, where we will likewise find a strange interplay between God and his angel.

In the famous story from Exodus 3, Moses is tending his flock on Mount Horeb when "the angel of the Lord appeared to him in a flame of fire out of a bush; he looked, and the bush was blazing, yet it was not consumed" (v. 2). Although you have likely heard this story before, you might not have noticed that Exodus tells us that it is an *angel* who appeared to Moses in the burning bush. It is easy to miss this detail, because if we go a little further into the story, we see that it is God himself who calls out from the bush: "Moses, Moses! . . .Come no closer! Remove the sandals from your feet, for the place on which you are standing is holy ground" (Ex 3:4–5). Indeed, for the remainder of this narrative, God is speaking to Moses directly, and in the course of the conversation, God even reveals his name—the holiest thing that is spoken in all of the Old Testament. The angel is never mentioned again. In fact, no other angels appear in the book of Exodus until chapter 14, when the angel of the Lord goes out before the people as they travel across the Red Sea (see Exodus 14:19).

Perhaps the mention of the angel in Exodus 3 seems no less perplexing than the angel-men who visit Abraham in Genesis 19, but even with just these two texts, we can see a pattern emerging. First, it is clear that angels can appear in different forms—as men in Genesis 19 or as a flame in Exodus 3.

Second, angels can speak for God in a very direct way, so much so that the angel of the Lord speaking or acting and the Lord himself speaking or acting can be referred to interchangeably in a single story. Lastly, something of the glory of God seems to be reflected in the angels, since Abraham can bow down and honor them, and they are often described with language of light or fire, like God himself.

Let us turn now to the New Testament to see if similar observations can be made about angels in the Nativity story. The angels show up in a great concentration during the events surrounding the birth of Christ, especially at the opening of Luke's gospel. Even for us today, it is at Christmastime more than any other that we see images of angels and think about them. At the very beginning of Luke 1, the angel Gabriel comes to Zechariah while he is serving in the Temple to tell him of Elizabeth's conception of John the Baptist:

> Then there appeared to him an angel of the Lord, standing at the right side of the altar of incense. When Zechariah saw him, he was terrified; and fear overwhelmed him. But the angel said to him, "Do not be afraid, Zechariah, for your prayer has been heard. Your wife Elizabeth will bear you a son, and you will name him John. You will have joy and gladness, and many will rejoice at his birth, for he will be great in the sight of the Lord. He must never drink wine or strong drink; even before

> his birth he will be filled with the Holy Spirit. (Lk 1:11–15)

Later in this passage, Gabriel identifies himself and tells Zechariah: "I am Gabriel. I stand in the presence of God" (v. 19). The angel Raphael says something very similar when he discloses his identity at the end of the book of Tobit: "I am Raphael, one of the seven angels who stand ready and enter before the glory of the Lord" (Tb 12:15). The similarity of Gabriel's introduction to that of Raphael is why we identify these two angels as "archangels," along with Michael (who is called an archangel in Jude 9).

Zechariah is overwhelmed by the presence of the angel, despite the fact that he serves in the Temple, where the Lord dwells. Clearly the appearance of the angel communicates something palpable of the glory of God that not even serving in the Temple has offered Zechariah. When Gabriel goes on to the Virgin Mary to announce to her that she will be the mother of Christ, she is likewise "much perplexed" by the angel's greeting and in awe of Gabriel, who tells her, "Do not be afraid" (Lk 1:29–30).

To add to these two appearances of Gabriel in the first chapter of Luke, in the very next chapter the whole host of heaven shows up. They announce the birth of Christ to the shepherds, singing, "Glory to God in the highest heaven, and on earth peace among those whom he favors!" (Lk 2:14). This is an incredibly striking scene. The hosts of heaven appear only twice in the Old Testament, and both times to prophets and in visions, not to a group of average Israelites and in person (see 1 Kings 22:19 and 2 Chronicles 18:18; Daniel 8:10). Just as Zechariah and Mary reacted to the angel Gabriel with fear and amazement, it is clear that this host of angels is awe-inspiring: "Then an angel of the Lord stood before them, and the glory of the Lord shone around them, and they were terrified. But the angel said to them, 'Do not be afraid'" (Lk 2:9–10).

These passages from the New Testament correspond well to some of the observations we made about angels in the Old Testament. Angels somehow reflect or show forth the glory of God (whatever their appearance), and they speak on God's behalf, announcing the most important and sacred things that God wants to communicate to humankind. But there is an additional puzzle piece offered by the Nativity story: the flurry of angelic activity surrounding the birth of Christ. Angels appear not only in the passages from Luke that we have just read but also in Matthew's gospel, where an angel announces the birth of Christ to Joseph (Mt 1:20) and an angel warns him in a dream to flee to Egypt (Mt 2:13). The angels seem to have a particularly close relationship with Christ, and Matthew's gospel refers to the angels as *Christ's* angels (cf. Mt 13:41, Mt 16:27, and Mt 24:31). It seems logical that if the angels speak on God's behalf and deliver his messages, they should be most intimately involved with God's greatest message to the world, the Word of God himself, Jesus Christ (cf. Jn 1:1). The angels continue to attend to Christ in a special way throughout his life—after his temptation by the devil (Mt 4:11; Mk 1:13), in the garden of Gethsemane before his Passion (Lk 22:43), and at his tomb on the morning of the Resurrection (Mt 28:2; Lk 24:4; Jn 20:12). If we see angels as speaking on God's behalf throughout the Bible, then the Incarnation—God's own speech—is the angel's big moment as well.

There are, of course, many other biblical passages in which angels appear, and they are certainly worth meditating upon. As we will see, the Church's teaching is drawn from such passages, and we will return to the Bible throughout the course of this book. By walking through a few of these stories in a preliminary way, however, you hopefully will be more alert to the mention of angels when you read the Bible and be on the lookout for when and how angels act. You can bring to bear these patterns that we have noticed to your own reading of both Old and New Testaments—that angels speak on God's behalf, even sometimes to the extent of being identified with him; that angels radiate with the glory of God and are sent from his presence; and that angels belong in a special way to Christ. All of these patterns will come into play as we turn to the Church's teaching on angels.

2.

WHAT DOES THE CHURCH TEACH ABOUT ANGELS?

In accord with the biblical evidence on angels, the Church's teaching on them—what we can know for certain and should hold with sure faith—is relatively modest. The *Catechism of the Catholic Church* dedicates nine sections to the angels in its teaching on creation (see §328–336), since angels are included in the article of faith where we profess that God made all things "visible and invisible." This part of the Creed is meant to affirm not simply a belief in material things that cannot be seen with the human eye (such as atoms or bacteria), but also a belief in created, spiritual realities such as the soul and the angels. The items that the *Catechism* puts forth as sure teaching on the angels are based on the biblical evidence, including what we have briefly surveyed.

First, the *Catechism* (§329) speaks about the word "angel" as indicating a job title, not a nature. In other words, "angel" describes what a celestial spirit *does*, not what it *is*; that is because the word "angel" comes from the Greek word *angelos*, which simply means "messenger." St. Augustine explains this point:

> The angels are spirits. When they are simply spirits, they are not angels, but when they are sent, they become angels; for "angel" is the name of a function not a nature. If you inquire about the nature of such beings, you find that they are spirits, if you ask what their office is, the answer is that they are angels. In respect of what they are, such creatures are spirits; in respect of what they do, they are angels. Make a comparison of human affairs. The name of someone's nature is "human being," the name of his job is "soldier." (*Expositions of the Psalms* 103.1.15, trans. Maria Boulding)

So the first and most important thing that we know about the angels is the job that God has given them in relation to us. It is interesting that the name we call the angels does not so much refer to who they are in themselves, but to who they are to *us*. We are using a relational word that is more like "mother" or "father" than a name like "Sarah" or "John" (although we do, of course, know some of the angels by name as well). This fact in and of itself indicates the love that the angels have for us and the service that they are willing to do for us. After all, in themselves the angels have no need to send messages to anyone. It is for our sakes that that they become messengers and servants—"Are not all angels spirits in the divine service, sent to serve for the sake of those who are to inherit salvation?" (Heb 1:14).

If the angels are messengers, we might ask what their message is. We already saw, of course, that the angels speak on God's behalf in all kinds of ways (to announce the birth of Isaac, the name of God, and so on). But the *Catechism* affirms a fact we hinted at in the previous chapter—that, fundamentally, the angels' message is the Incarnation. They play an integral role in salvation history, and that history points toward and culminates in God becoming man in Jesus Christ. Jesus is called the "Word" of God (Jn 1:1), his "power" and "wisdom" (1 Cor 1:24), and according to the church fathers, he is the one referred to in the Old Testament as the "angel of great counsel" (Is 9:6 in their translation, the Septuagint). The fathers do not use this title to imply that Jesus is a celestial spirit or that he is not fully God; rather, they use it to describe Christ as the greatest messenger of all, because he is God's message in the flesh. Let us hear from Augustine again:

> In Latin, in fact, "angels" are "heralds." If Christ had had nothing to announce, he would not be called an angel. He exhorted us to believe, and by faith to lay hold of eternal life; he announced something present, foretold something to come in the future. Insofar as he announced something present, he was an angel; insofar as he foretold something to come, he was a prophet; insofar as

> the Word was made flesh (Jn 1:14), he was the Lord of both angels and prophets. (*Homily on John* 24.7, trans. Edmund Hill)

Jesus is the chief angel because he is the supreme messenger, announcing God's saving plan and also *being* God's saving plan. Jesus is, so to speak, king of the angels and the king angel. This shared mission of Christ and his angels explains the angelic activity surrounding the birth of Christ, their continued ministry to him, and the reference to the angels as "Christ's angels" that we noted in the previous chapter. It especially makes sense that the angels who made so many announcements during the time of the old covenant would get to make the big announcement, that of Christ's birth to Mary and of his precursor, John the Baptist.

The fact that the angels belong to Christ and that they are messengers of his mission also corresponds to the fact that angels continue to help and aid Christ's Church today. The Church, after all, is Christ's body, his continued mystical presence on earth. Just as the angels prepared the coming of Christ and ministered to his body while he walked the earth, so they continue to minister to his body the Church. The *Catechism* goes so far as to say that "the whole life of the Church benefits from the mysterious and powerful help of angels" (*CCC* §334). The *Catechism* also points out two specific ways in which angelic aid is given to the Church: through their guardianship and protection (which we will cover in chapter

3) and through their participation in the liturgy (which we will cover in chapter 4).

Apart from the angels' role in salvation history and their relationship to us, the *Catechism* also teaches, regarding the angels in themselves, that they are "purely spiritual creatures" and that they "have intelligence and will: they are personal and immortal creatures, surpassing in perfection all visible creatures, as the splendor of their glory bears witness" (*CCC* §330). This one line puts forth a number of statements about the angels that need to be more fully explained.

When the *Catechism* refers to angels as "spiritual," it is not suggesting that the angels have a good spiritual life, that they pray a lot, or whatever else might come to mind when we use the word "spiritual" today. Although the angels *do* have a perfect spiritual life in the modern sense of the word, what the *Catechism* is expressing is that the angels do not have bodies, that they are not corporeal—they are not made up of "stuff" that occupies physical space (flesh and bones and blood as we are). They are spirit, as the Bible often describes them (for some examples, see Daniel 3:86; Wisdom 7:23; 2 Maccabees 3:24; Matthew 8:16; Revelation 1:4). If you find this difficult to imagine, you are not alone. Many in the ancient world thought of angels as having something like a body of air or fire (that is, something that has a tangible existence but is not "stuff" per se). And since angels manifest their presence with light (e.g., Lk 2:9) and fire (e.g., Heb 1:7) and wind (e.g.,

Ez 1:4–5), this idea makes good sense. But deeper reflection on the nature of creation led the Church to confess that angels are truly *incorporeal* and purely spiritual. After all, the unique character of a human being is to be both spiritual and corporeal, to have both body and soul, and so if the angels were described in exactly the same way, they too would be human. Just as the animals below us are bodily but not spiritual, so the angels above us are spiritual but not bodily. The incorporeality of the angels also makes it easy to explain how they can appear in such varied ways, from something as ethereal as fire to something as concrete as a human being. When we say that angels are "in" a certain place, we mean that they are acting in that place, not that their body is located there. Since the angels' power is not infinite like God's, they can act only in one place at a time, thus being in some sense present in one place and not in another.

The most obvious question that might arise from the Church's definition of the angels is this: how can angels appear if they do not have bodies? Augustine explains that angels, as spiritual beings, can discern the makeup of the universe much better than we can and are able to manipulate it and put it to their own use in a way that surpasses our understanding. Thomas Aquinas also contends that angels can reside in a body for a time in order to be seen and touched. Although this assumption of a body is not like that of Christ in the Incarnation—because we know that God *becomes* man in

Christ rather than simply *assuming* a body—nevertheless, it is still an act of charity for the angels to walk among us in this way.

This fact that we have now established, that angels are incorporeal, also explains why they are immortal. To die does not mean, even in the case of human beings, to cease to exist, since the human soul lives on after death and will be reunited with its body at the resurrection. Rather, death is a dis-integration of the body in that the soul is no longer able to give life to the body and operate it; the soul-body unity has broken down and ceased to function. Since angels have no bodies, they cannot experience death; that is, they cannot experience the separation of soul and body. Saying that angels are immortal, however, is not the same as saying that they are eternal (which means without beginning or end). Only God is eternal, though the angels (and us along with them!) have the capacity to live forever with God in heaven.

So if the angels are incorporeal and immortal, what does it mean to say that they are personal, and that they have a mind and a will like us? Although the angels do not have bodies, they are still individuals. Just as we have a soul that can be distinguished from any other soul (even though the soul itself is not bodily), so also with the angels. We therefore can say that each angel is a person. This way of speaking, of course, might sound a little odd, since we are used to speaking only about human persons. Nevertheless, the angels are every bit as individual as any human being. They have their own proper thoughts, actions, and life. We can see this clearly enough in the handful of named angels in the Bible who appear, act, and identify themselves.

Lastly, the *Catechism* affirms that the angels are more perfect than we are. The way in which they cooperate with God and radiate his glory throughout the Bible testifies to this fact. But this inequality hardly seems fair, given that we are stuck with these fleshly bodies and death! Why would God make angels in his image and then also human beings, if we are lesser? Thomas Aquinas has an article dedicated to this question in his *Summa Theologiae* (see I.93.3). There he asks, "Is the image of God in angels more than in man?" to which he answers yes, but in a qualified way. Since we primarily image God by being rational creatures and not in our bodies (in other words, we don't *physically* look like God, but we imitate him by use of our minds), then the angels have us beat. Their intellect is higher—they can learn about God without looking at any physical thing, for example (they don't have eyes, after all!). But God in his infinite wisdom creates many good things, ordered properly and reflecting the divine in different ways. So human beings image God in some ways that the angels cannot; for example, that one human being is born from another shows forth that God in his inner life proceeds as God from God (as we say in the Creed about the Son). That is, in our common humanity we can reflect to a certain degree that God is Trinity.

Another way in which we uniquely image God is that our souls are present to our whole bodies without being split up or spread out. This mysterious presence of the soul is analogous to the way in which God can be present to the whole world. In other words, we image and show forth a spiritual presence in a corporeal reality. So, in a primary way, the angels are more perfect than us, but in order for God to show forth his own beauty and perfection, he creates many kinds of creatures capable of reflecting different aspects of his life.

We have now established what the Church teaches about angels, which, put simply, is this: angels are rational, incorporeal spirits, created by God in his image to share his life and to be in communion with us. Over this last point we have passed rather quickly, however. In what ways can angels be said to help us, and what sort of communion do we have with them now? We will look at this question more deeply in the next two chapters, as we think about guardian angels and angelic participation in the liturgy.

3.

WHAT IS A GUARDIAN ANGEL, AND DO I HAVE ONE?

On the guardianship of the angels, the *Catechism* quotes Basil the Great (ca. 330–379), who says, "No one will deny every believer has an angel that accompanies him, acting like a kind of pedagogue and shepherd and directing his life" (*Against Eunomius* 3.1, trans. M. DelCogliano and A. Radde-Gallwitz). Basil's confidence in the existence of guardian angels reflects that it is a very ancient belief and consistent throughout Church tradition. This belief comes directly from the Bible, which mentions angels as having the role of guardian and protector. Take, for example, these two well-known passages from the Psalms:

> The angel of the Lord encamps
> around those who fear him, and delivers them.
> (Ps 34:7)

> For he will command his angels concerning you
> to guard you in all your ways.

> On their hands they will bear you up,
> so that you will not dash your foot against a stone.
> You will tread on the lion and the adder,
> the young lion and the serpent you will trample under foot. (Ps 91:11–13)

These passages, however, speak of the guardianship of angels over God's people in a general way. That each *individual* in some way has an angel is implied in Jesus's statement at the beginning of the parable of the lost sheep in Matthew's gospel: "Take care that you do not despise one of these little ones; for, I tell you, in heaven their angels continually see the face of my Father in heaven" (18:10). Jesus underscores the value of every one of his sheep by saying that each "little one" has an angel who is now seeing God face-to-face. The guardianship of the angels is also seen clearly in the book of Tobit, where the angel Raphael is the companion of Tobias, helping him and guiding him throughout his journey. Moreover, in the book of Acts, when Peter miraculously escapes from prison (with the help of an angel) and is at the door, the faithful within do not believe that it is him and instead say, "It is his angel!" (Acts 12:15). These biblical passages do not offer a very thorough explanation about the protection of angels, but they indicate that from the time of the writing of the New Testament, Christians already believed in individual guardian angels.

Although the Bible does not give us a lot of information about the function of guardian angels, one frequent image used by the church fathers (such as by Basil above) is that of a shepherd or herdsman—keeping the sheep on the right course. This image resonates with Christ's words in Matthew 18:10 quoted above; the context of that quotation, after all, is the parable of the lost sheep. Eusebius of Caesarea (ca. 260–339), for example, uses the image when he writes: "Surely the All-Good, the King of kings, the Supreme, God Almighty, that the men on earth might not be like brute beasts without rulers and guardians, set over them the holy angels to be their leaders and governors like herdsmen and shepherds, and set over all, and made the head of all His Only-begotten and First-born Word" (*Demonstration of the Gospel* 4.6, trans. William Ferrar).

Eusebius conjures up a wonderful image of Christ as the Good Shepherd with his fleet of angelic sheepdogs gathering us into the fold through the narrow gate. It also recalls our previous discussion of Christ as head of the angels, the "angel of great counsel." This parallel between shepherd and angel makes good sense if we remember that priests and bishops are likewise compared to shepherds. Like human beings, angels can participate in God's plan by caring for and guiding his people. This job of the angels to "herd" us applies especially to our souls at death; the angels are understood to be our heavenly escorts. For example, after Lazarus dies—in the story of Lazarus and the rich man found in Luke 16—he is "carried away by the angels to be with Abraham" (Lk 16:22). The church fathers, following this story (but also in accord with the ancient worldview about spirits generally), believed in the assistance of angels in guiding the soul to paradise. John Chrysostom, in a homily on this story, asks, "If we need a guide in passing from one city to another, how much more will the soul which . . . is moving toward the life to come need guides to lead it?" (*Homily on Lazarus* 2.2, trans. Catharine Roth). In a similar vein, in Jude 9 the archangel Michael "contended with the devil and disputed about the body of Moses," implying his guardianship at Moses's death. To this day, prayers for the dead and Masses for the dead often invoke the intercession of angels, such as the *in paradisum* prayer, which also recalls the story of Lazarus: "May the angels lead you into paradise; may the martyrs receive you at your arrival and lead you to the holy city Jerusalem. May choirs of angels receive you and with Lazarus, once a poor man, may you have eternal rest."

In addition to this idea of a guardian angel as a shepherd or herdsman, there are various other roles attributed to these angels by different church fathers—that they can bring peace, that they can turn us to repentance, and that they can help us to pray. Primarily, however, these angels are seen as guardians in spiritual warfare against the devil and *his* angels, that is, the angels who took the devil's part and so are the devil's messengers (more about them will be said in chapter 7). This aspect of guardianship is the one most in view in Thomas Aquinas's *Summa Theologiae*. Of the constancy of this angelic protection, Thomas says: "The demons are ever assailing us, according to 1 Peter 5:8: 'Your adversary the devil, as a roaring lion, goeth about, seeking whom he may devour.' Much more therefore do the good angels ever guard us" (*ST* I.113.6, trans. Laurence Shapcote). Exactly how and why the angels perform these actions (and when and why they do *not* intervene) remains largely mysterious. Their work is always in accord with the providence of God, after all, and divine providence is often quite inscrutable in our lives.

Since angels do not have bodies, we ought to envision this battle as a spiritual one, and the battle is one we might primarily conceive of as pertaining to proper worship. The demons are always trying to steal the honor due to God for themselves, whereas angels are always trying to get us to worship God and honor him as they do—not only with ritual acts of worship but also with all the acts of our body and all the motivations of our hearts (the involvement of angels in worship will be the subject of the next chapter).

The guardianship of angels, however, extends far beyond the idea of an individual protector or helper, as we have already noted above. Ancient people, regardless of their religious faith, took for granted that the world was full of mediating spirits, and early Christians likewise understood angels as protectors in a much wider sense. In the book of Revelation, John writes letters to the angels of each of the seven churches (see Revelation 2–3). The fathers took this address to mean that each church also has a guardian angel. From certain Old Testament passages (e.g., Dt 32:8 in the Septuagint), they understood that each nation has an angel, especially tasked with leading its people closer to God in the time of the old covenant. The archangel Michael was thought by some to be the guardian angel of the nation of Israel, perhaps further explaining the mention in Jude of the disputation over Moses's body; the guardian angel of Israel would naturally have a special interest in Moses! Of this guardianship Pseudo-Dionysius (who wrote sometime in the fifth or sixth century) says, "The Word of God has assigned our Hierarchy to Angels, by naming Michael as Ruler of the Jewish people, and others over other nations. For the Most High established borders of nations according to number of Angels of God" (*Celestial Hierarchy* 9.2, trans. John Parker).

Early Christians also understood angels to be guardians and transmitters of the Mosaic law, a belief reflected in Galatians 3:19: "Why then the law? It was added because of transgressions, until the offspring would come to whom the promise had been made; and it was ordained through angels by a mediator." In short, just as God works through multitudes of human beings simultaneously to achieve his plan and just as we can cooperate in guiding others to him, so also do the angels participate in this work of salvation according to their own nature and abilities.

Unfortunately, belief in guardian angels has sometimes led to superstition or drawn Christians into magical practices, such as invoking the names of angels as if they had some secret power. Although the angels can represent God in their person, they are nevertheless not to be worshipped in themselves—as the book of Revelation makes clear. When John is overcome by the glory of the angel's vision, he says, "Then I fell down at his feet to worship him, but he said to me, 'You must not do that! I am a fellow servant with you and your comrades who hold the testimony of Jesus. Worship God! For the testimony of Jesus is the spirit of prophecy'" (Rv 19:10). Angelic aid and protection are a means of unity with God, not a replacement for God. Anyone—even one who appears to be an angel of light (cf. 2 Cor 11:14)—who preaches a different gospel or demands worship is not an angel of God. Superstitions regarding the angels have been around since the earliest days of the faith, when some Christians would read magical spells or incantations that invoked the names of angels (John Chrysostom, for example, chastises his congregation for participating in such rituals). Augustine was also concerned about these practices and with the similar practice of astrology. He urges his congregation to think of angels as faithful stewards of the house of God, rather than as those whom we can bribe to get around the normal rules of prayer to gain some special favor. On this point Augustine says:

> It's not only though, if some human being, but also if any angel, seemingly, should wish to tempt you, either through some kind of apparition or through

> a dream and say, "Do this for me, celebrate this rite for me, because I am"—for example—"the angel Gabriel"; don't believe him. As for you, stick safely to worshiping the one God, who is Father and Son and Holy Spirit. If it's really an angel, he will rejoice at your worshiping like that; but if he gets angry because you haven't given him something extra, then you must now understand him to be the one about whom the apostle says that he "transforms himself into an angel of light" (2 Cor 11:14). He wants to block your way, he is intruding himself with evil intent; he is not the mediator who reconciles, but rather the one who separates. . . . That is not the kind of great household that our Lord runs. His servants love him, his children love him. If you want to corrupt any of them, as it were, on the side, in order to be admitted to their master, you will be expelled very far indeed from that great household. (*Sermon* 198.48, trans. Edmund Hill)

Modern practices that have tended in this superstitious direction were commented upon by the Vatican's Congregation for Divine Worship in 2001 in a document titled *Directory on Popular Piety and the Liturgy*. In §217 the document notes that "popular devotion to the Holy Angels, which is legitimate and good, can, however, also give rise to possible deviations." It mentions three such deviations:

1. Imagining that the world is in a constant state of cosmological struggle, an "incessant battle between good and evil spirits, or Angels and daemons, in which man is left at the mercy of superior forces and over which he is helpless." This is not the message of the Gospel, which proclaims that the devil was defeated by Christ and that the Christian has the power, by grace, to resist the devil through moral actions, prayers, the sacraments, and so on.
2. Attributing every good or bad thing that happens in life to the actions of a guardian angel or a demon (think of the popular caricature of an angel and a demon sitting on someone's shoulder and competing for their attention).
3. The practice of assigning names to angels (including guardian angels), except, of course, the angels whose names we know from scripture. Although the document does not give a reason for discouraging this practice, one can imagine that naming your guardian angel or seeking out an angel's name could be a dangerous form of curiosity or could be seen as an attempt to gain power over an angel as if—as Augustine puts it—an angel could be corrupted or bribed on the side.

Out of similar concerns to those listed by the *Directory*, we will not here address the many personal revelations of the saints regarding their guardian angels, nor people who have had visions or communications with their angel (such as Aloysius Gonzaga and Padre Pio). Such stories may very well be authentic (and in the cases of canonized saints, we would give them the benefit of the doubt), and these experiences can also be edifying for the person who has had them. These experiences do not, however, belong to the deposit of faith, in the sense that they are not *public* revelation intended for the reflection of all the faithful. God continues to work in our lives and through his angels, and we may have had some personal experience or devotion to them that has been meaningful to us. But we must be careful not to universalize such experiences, nor to put an emphasis on them that makes it appear as if they supersede or add to the public revelation of God in Jesus Christ, as recorded in the gospels and witnessed in Church tradition. John of the Cross wisely reminds us that

> in giving us his Son, his only Word (for he possesses no other), he spoke everything to us at once in this sole Word—and he has no more to say . . . because what he spoke before to the prophets in parts, he has now spoken all at once by giving us the All Who is His Son. Any person questioning God or desiring some vision or revelation would be guilty not only of foolish behaviour but also of offending him, by not fixing his eyes entirely upon

> Christ and by living with the desire for some other novelty. (*CCC* §65)

This warning is not meant to throw cold water on our love of angels and our devotion to our guardian angel, which can be healthy and fruitful (and will be further discussed in chapter 6). Rather, it is meant to draw our attention to what is authoritative regarding the angels and what is of secondary importance.

In conclusion, we know from the Bible and the tradition of the church fathers that we all have angels guarding us and protecting us, as our fellow citizens in the heavenly Jerusalem. They assist God in guiding us (and the Church and the nations) toward him, and we can be assured of that assistance. One place, in particular, where we may become aware of the presence of angels and come into friendship with them is in the liturgy, the topic to which we will now turn.

4.

DO THE ANGELS PARTICIPATE IN THE LITURGY?

No book of the Bible stirs the imagination about angelic activity as much as its very last: Revelation. In this book, we have a glimpse of the heavenly Jerusalem and see what the angels are doing when at home, so to speak. What they are doing is worshipping God. Like the prophet Ezekiel, who sees a vision of God borne on his heavenly chariot with the four living creatures (see Ezekiel 1:4–5), John has a vision in which he witnesses living creatures worshipping God in heaven:

> Around the throne, and on each side of the throne, are four living creatures, full of eyes in front and behind: the first living creature like a lion, the second living creature like an ox, the third living creature with a face like a human face, and the fourth living creature like a flying eagle. And the four living creatures, each of them with six wings, are full of eyes all around and inside. Day and night without ceasing they sing,

> "Holy, holy, holy,
> the Lord God the Almighty,
> who was and is and is to come."
>
> And whenever the living creatures give glory and honor and thanks to the one who is seated on the throne, who lives forever and ever, the twenty-four elders fall before the one who is seated on the throne and worship the one who lives forever and ever; they cast their crowns before the throne, singing,
>
> "You are worthy, our Lord and God,
> to receive glory and honor and power,
> for you created all things,
> and by your will they existed and were created." (Rv 4:6–11)

The book of Revelation has many other scenes involving heavenly worship that are described very much like a divine liturgy, with features in common with our practice of the Mass today. These include prayers offered like incense (8:4), a heavenly altar (8:3–5, 14:18), golden vessels (15:7), the reading from a scroll (5:1), the sacrifice of the Lamb (5:6), and praise offered in song (4:8, 4:11). The future destiny of the world is also envisioned as liturgical in Revelation—the conclusion of history is the wedding feast of the Lamb (19:6–9, 21:2), and heaven is the new Jerusalem, in which God himself is the Temple (21:22–23). The angels are intimately involved in these liturgical proceedings throughout the book.

What do we make of this imagery? Do angels participate in the Mass, and if they do, how do we conceive of it? First, we should note that it is clear from the Old Testament that earthly worship is reflective of or patterned on the liturgy of heaven. Revelation draws on this idea, of course, but the letter to the Hebrews discusses it more fully, explaining that Israel's Temple worship is based on heavenly worship. It goes further, however, showing that in the new covenant, after the veil in the Temple has been torn and Christ has ascended into heaven, we no longer have merely the shadow of heavenly worship; rather, Jesus has entered into heaven itself to intercede for us:

> Now the main point in what we are saying is this: we have such a high priest, one who is seated at the right hand of the throne of the Majesty in the heavens, a minister in the sanctuary and the true tent that the Lord, and not any mortal, has set up. For every high priest is appointed to offer gifts and sacrifices; hence it is necessary for this priest also to have something to offer. Now if he were on earth, he would not be a priest at all, since there are priests who offer gifts according to the law. They offer worship in a sanctuary that is a sketch and shadow of the heavenly one; for Moses, when he was about to erect the tent, was warned, "See that you make everything according to the pattern that was shown you on the mountain." But Jesus has now obtained a more excellent ministry, and to

> that degree he is the mediator of a better covenant, which has been enacted through better promises. (Heb 8:1–6)

In other words, Moses set up the original tabernacle in imitation of heavenly things, a "sketch and shadow" of them, patterned after what God revealed to him (on this pattern, see especially Exodus 25–27). The worship of God's people, then, has always reflected the liturgy of heaven. What has changed is that now Christ has ascended from earth into heaven, and he presides as priest in the heavenly temple—the tent (or tabernacle) that no man has set up, as Hebrews refers to it. Christian worship, then, is not a mere imitation of the heavenly liturgy but is now swept up into the real thing. Christ was sacrificed once for all, and the Mass is a participation in that perfect sacrifice, which is offered by the perfect priest, mediator, and victim in heaven.

So, if when we celebrate Mass we are caught up into and join the liturgy of heaven, we should perhaps not speak so much of the angels participating in our liturgy but about us participating in *theirs* (although of course it becomes ours now and will be so perfectly when we reach the beatific vision). This sense of the Mass as participation in the worship of heaven was present from very early on in the Church's tradition. For example, the Roman Canon—which is an ancient Eucharistic prayer, dating to the seventh century with parts that are much older—requests angelic aid in the liturgy. In the modern translation, this prayer asks "that these gifts be borne by the hands of your holy angel to your altar on high in the sight of your divine majesty, so that all of us, who through this participation at the altar receive the most holy Body and Blood of your Son, may be filled with every grace and heavenly blessing." Here it is assumed that the sacrifice of the altar on earth is brought up into the heavenly temple and that an angel is involved in this meeting of heaven and earth in worship. It is because of this connection that the Eucharist is effective ("so that all of us . . . may be filled," as the prayer says), because this sacrifice is a participation in the unique sacrifice of the Body and Blood of Christ, who is now seated in heaven at the right hand of the Father. This angelic involvement in the Eucharistic sacrifice has sometimes been represented by decorating Eucharistic tabernacles with images of angels, a practice that also parallels the placement of the golden cherubim upon the ark of the covenant, with their wings spread out to overshadow it (see Exodus 25:18–20).

But perhaps the place where it is most obvious that we are joining in the praise of the angels at Mass is when we sing the Sanctus. The word *sanctus* is Latin for "holy" and refers to the part of the Mass when we sing the song of the seraphim heard by Isaiah: "Holy, holy, holy is the LORD of hosts; the whole earth is full of his glory" (Is 6:3; it is also heard by John in a slightly different version, cited above—see Revelation 4:8). This prayer sums up the praise of the heavenly court and expresses the only thing that really needs to be said to God. Because after all the struggles of this life have ceased, we will have no more petitions, no more intercessions. When there is a new heaven and a new earth, God's presence within it will be palpable and transparent; it will indeed be full of his glory. So at this precious moment in the liturgy when we prepare to receive the Lord in the Eucharist, we praise him as we will when we see him face-to-face. We praise him now in time in the same way that we will praise him in eternity, just as the angels do. In the Liturgy of St. John Chrysostom (one of the divine liturgies celebrated by Eastern Catholics and Eastern Orthodox), communicants ask even more explicitly to imitate the angels, singing, "Let us who mystically represent the cherubim and sing the thrice-holy hymn to the life-creating Trinity, now set aside all earthly cares." Indeed, for at least that moment of praise in the Sanctus, we do set aside our earthly cares and imitate the angels, whose only care is praise of the Lord.

These two moments—the prayer of the Roman Canon and the Sanctus—are the two angelic moments of the Mass highlighted in the *Catechism* (see *CCC* §335). But just as the church fathers understood the guardianship of angels to extend far beyond the individual guardianship of souls, so also they saw angelic participation as a constant feature in the rites of the Church. This idea we already saw in the *Catechism*'s statement that "the whole life of the Church benefits from the mysterious and powerful help of angels" (§334). And what is more at the heart of the Church's life than her liturgy and sacraments? The fathers saw this angelic help as present from the get-go, so to speak, at baptism. In the Sacrament of Baptism, after all, we join the family of God, of which the angels are a part; they are our older and wiser siblings. The fathers universally imagine angels watching and rejoicing over the baptism of each Christian, and some even see the angel as an attendant of the baptism (this is sometimes shown in ancient images of Jesus's baptism, where the angels await him on the shore).

This association of the angels with baptism means that, of course, they take special delight in the proceedings of the Easter Vigil. Cyril of Jerusalem (ca. 313–386) helps the candidates for Baptism envision the angelic presence on that special night, saying:

> Then, may you receive Christ's name and the power of things divine. Even now, I beseech you, in spirit lift up your eyes; behold the angelic choirs, and the Lord of all, God, on His throne, with the Son, the Only-begotten, sitting on His right hand, and the Spirit, too, and the Thrones and Dominations ministering, and every man of you and every woman receiving salvation. Even now let there ring in your ears that excellent sound which you shall hear when the Angels, celebrating your salvation, chant: "Blessed are they whose iniquities are forgiven," on the day when, like new stars of

> the Church, you will enter, your bodies bright, your souls shining. (*Procatechesis* 15, trans. Leo P. McCauley)

If we here on earth rejoice so much at baptisms—we who see the divine reality through earthly signs and sacraments—how much more the angels, who can perceive the spiritual reality directly, without a veil?

The church fathers also imagine the angels flocking to Mass, especially the guardian angels, accompanying the souls whom they protect. Origen says, then, that we have a twofold church at every celebration, one angelic and one human (see *Homilies on Luke* 23). Paul seems to have in mind a similar angelic presence in the liturgy when he recommends that women cover their heads "because of the angels" (1 Cor 11:10). The angels love both the Liturgy of the Word and the Liturgy of the Eucharist. Although angels have no need to read the scriptures because they see the Word of God himself, nonetheless they delight in the Word proclaimed for our salvation. As for the Liturgy of the Eucharist, John Chrysostom reflects on the angels' attention and even participation in the events on the altar: "Angels are then present with the priest, and the whole tribune and space around the altar is filled with heavenly powers in honour of Him that is there" (*On the Priesthood* 6.4, trans. B. Harris Cowper).

All of this angelic attendance at the liturgy makes a lot of sense when we understand that there is only one worship of the one true God. In the beatific vision this unity of God's people before his throne will be utterly clear, but even now we join the angels in paying homage to the only one who is to be worshipped. There is but one sacrifice of the Church both in heaven and on earth. Augustine helps us to imagine this, giving us a picture of human beings traveling here below and the angels cheering us on:

> It is very right that these blessed and immortal spirits, who inhabit celestial dwellings, and rejoice in the communications of their creator's fullness, firm in his eternity, assured in his truth, holy by his grace, since they compassionately and tenderly regard us miserable mortals, and wish us to become immortal and happy, do not desire us to sacrifice to themselves, but to him whose sacrifice they know to be in common with us. For we and they together are in the city of God . . . the human part sojourning here below, the angelic aiding from above. (*City of God* X.7, trans. Marcus Dods)

5.

DO THE ANGELS HAVE RANKS?

In our discussion thus far, we have already mentioned many different designations used for the angels as they appear in scripture. What do these names mean, and do they indicate anything about the structure of heaven? In various passages, scripture seems to be describing different kinds of angels—cherubim (for some examples, see Genesis 3:24; Exodus 37:7–9; 2 Kings 19:15; Daniel 3:54; Sirach 49:8; Hebrews 9:5), seraphim (Is 6:2), and archangels (1 Thes 4:16; Jude 9), as well as thrones, dominions, principalities, and powers (see Colossians 1:16; Ephesians 1:21). The Bible does not give us much data about what these words might mean with respect to the angelic court. Correspondingly, although we know from scripture that there *are* types of angels, opinions about the meaning of these ranks of angels are not *de fide* (i.e., they are not a sure part of the deposit of the faith, and we are not required to accept these opinions). These considerations fall squarely within the realm of speculative theology. Nevertheless, there are old traditions regarding these ranks of the angels that build upon divine revelation.

Much of the received tradition regarding the ranks of angels derives from Pseudo-Dionysius (we have already quoted from him once before), who styled himself in his writing as *the* Dionysius the Areopagite mentioned in Acts 17:34. His works, especially *The Celestial Hierarchy*, are highly influential on the subject of angels. In the West, these traditions about the angels reach a kind of codification in the *Summa* of Thomas Aquinas, which dedicates eight articles to the discussion of the angelic hierarchy (see *ST* I.108). What follows is a general summary of Thomas's teaching, which is in turn a distillation of the tradition that came before him.

First, Thomas notes that absolutely speaking there is only one hierarchy of both human beings and angels under their one king, who is God. All creatures made in the image of God are meant to serve and worship him together. But in a second sense, one can think of a hierarchy of rational creatures according to the way in which they know. That is because, as we noted in chapter 2, the primary way in which we image God is in our intellectual nature. Taking their inspiration from Wisdom 11:20 ("you have arranged all things by measure and number and weight"), many theologians, especially in the medieval tradition, focus on contemplating the ordering of the universe and trying to discern how God has issued forth every kind of perfection therein. For this reason (that of creating every kind of perfection), as we saw above, God created both rational creatures without bodies (the angels) and rational creatures with bodies (human beings). In this line of thinking, even among the angels we might also be able to discern a manifold reflection of the perfection of God.

This varied reflection, according to Thomas Aquinas, has to do with angelic knowledge. Why would the distinction in the ranks of angels have to do with knowledge and not with glory or status or something of that kind? Since angels do not have bodies, the distinctions between them must somehow derive from their intellectual nature; thus this interest in degrees of knowledge. The first thing to understand about angelic knowledge is that it is different from human knowledge. As human beings, we gain knowledge from looking at particular things in the world and then coming to a greater understanding of how those things fit together. For example, we can only learn to identify a certain kind of tree by looking at many different examples of that tree and particular things about it (its bark, its leaf shape, etc.). By gaining all that particular knowledge, we come to a more general knowledge of the type of tree—say, an oak or a pine—and can subsequently recognize that this tree is an oak and that one is a pine. This process is *not* how an angel comes to know things. For an angel, who is purely spiritual and intellectual, it is more natural to come at things in the exact opposite way. Angels conceive of general truths first (of the universal causes of things, of general categories, and so on);

they do not need to arrive at truths through particular things that they observe with their senses (given that they have none).

So rational creatures are arrayed on an ascending scale of knowledge, coming to know more or less according to their nature and their different capacities. How should we think of this, and why does it matter that God creates different beings that fill up this ascending scale of knowledge? As an analogy, let us consider a football game. The players in the game have different scopes of knowledge and fields of influence, so to speak. The wide receiver is concerned with a very specific task and needs awareness of only those things that pertain to receiving the football, should it come his way. His mind is focused on catching the ball. The quarterback must have a broader scope of knowledge of the game, a more comprehensive view of the "general causes" of football—what actions to take, when and where and how they unfold. His mind is focused on making the play. The coach must have a broader and more general understanding of the game still, knowing how all the pieces fall into place and how all the players must interact; his knowledge even extends to things like recruiting players. His mind is focused on winning the game. Without each person on this ascending scale of knowledge, there would be no football game. So also we can think of rational creatures as having an ascending scale of knowledge and sphere of influence. Without each and every one of them, there would be no well-ordered universe. In the analogy, the highest angel would be like the coach, a lower one like the quarterback, and a lower one still like the wide receiver. God does not figure in the analogy—he would have to be something like the inventor of football, of all its rules and its joys.

More specifically, then, Thomas divides the angels into three general hierarchies. The first hierarchy has the highest form of knowledge, knowing things in God and connected immediately with him (they contemplate the final end of all things). This group is like the football coach. The second hierarchy is a little lower, concerned with the general causes that order all things to their end in God. This group is like the quarterback. The third hierarchy is concerned with the particulars that find their end in God. They are like the wide receiver. This third group is the one that is directly engaged in human affairs. Since angels know things from their universal causes in any case, what this means about the third group is that although they are in some sense "lower," in another sense they have more knowledge than the other groups, insofar as they are given knowledge of all the particulars on earth, such as people whom they are going to guard and send messages to.

So far so good. Angels are arrayed in a hierarchy displaying different perfections of their intellectual nature, but how are the angels mentioned in scripture aligned with this threefold hierarchy? Speculation about these assignments is made according to the following logic. The ones assigned to the highest tier are those whose names seem to be related to God himself; thus it was reasoned that they had the first kind of knowledge. These are the *seraphim* (which means "fiery ones," as God is a consuming fire), *cherubim* (a word related to the worship of God but also thought to refer to fullness of knowledge), and *thrones* (upon which God is seated). To the middle rank are assigned the angels whose names seem to have something to do with the general governance of things (and therefore associated with general causes): *dominions, virtues*, and *powers*. In the third hierarchy—those concerned with particulars—we have the angels whose names imply an active work: *principalities, archangels*, and *angels*. The specific ordering of "dominions, virtues, powers, and principalities" is inspired by Paul's ordering of angelic names in Ephesians 1:21. These nine groups, then—seraphim, cherubim, thrones, dominions, virtues, powers, principalities, archangels, and angels—constitute what are sometimes referred to as the nine choirs of angels.

If you find this foray into angelology a little dizzying, fear not! It is not incumbent upon the faithful Catholic to believe in this hierarchical arrangement of the angels, nor to understand it. This speculation springs from a desire to praise God, whose wisdom "orders all things well" (Ws 8:1), and to savor the hints left to us in scripture about the angelic life. Such intellectual efforts can be salutary, as long as we do not get too attached to our human conclusions or distracted by these things that are not a part of God's public revelation. But there are many other, less heady ways to cultivate a healthy devotion to the angels, and these will be the topic of the next chapter.

6.

HOW CAN I BE MORE DEVOTED TO THE ANGELS?

According to Augustine, the command to love God and neighbor includes our celestial neighbors, the angels (see *On Christian Teaching* 1.31). In what way can we love them or have our spiritual life informed by their presence? The *Directory on Popular Piety and the Liturgy* from the Congregation for Divine Worship, mentioned in chapter 3, makes a few suggestions about the characteristics manifested by someone who has a healthy relationship with the angels. These suggestions will help get us started in thinking about devotion to the angels. They are:

- devout gratitude to God for having placed these heavenly spirits of great sanctity and dignity at the service of man;
- an attitude of devotion deriving from the knowledge of living constantly in the presence of the Holy Angels of God;

- serenity and confidence in facing difficult situations, since the Lord guides and protects the faithful in the way of justice through the ministry of His Holy Angels (§216).

These dispositions are wonderfully expressed; the presence of angels in our lives should result in increased gratitude, piety, and serenity. There are many ways that we can love the angels, but let us take these three effects of angelic devotion as a starting point to identify the areas of our lives where we might be more conscious of the angels, imitate them, or invoke their intercession.

The first effect of proper devotion to the angels is gratitude. Knowing even a little about the angelic way of life from the previous chapters should make us stand in awe that such creatures willingly and lovingly serve us and help bring us to God. We should always be conscious to give thanks to God for the holy examples he has put in our lives, and we can add the angels to that list. Perhaps we can learn more about the disposition of gratitude from the angels, because gratitude is an angel's main line of business. Angels do not have any delusions about themselves stemming from sin; they are not jealous or insecure. They can give God his due always and with joy. Their whole life is an act of praise, of giving thanks. It is no surprise, then, that the celebration of the Eucharist (a word that comes from the Greek verb *eucharisteo* and means "to give thanks") is the correlate on earth to the worship in heaven.

There are also other specific instances when the angels accompany us or aid us in our thanksgiving. For example, the Morning Prayer of the Divine Office is called "Lauds," which comes from the Latin verb *laudere* and means "to praise." This time of prayer in particular is thought to occur in the presence of the angels, as implied in Psalm 138:1 (as the Latin Bible has it: "I will praise thee, O Lord, with my whole heart: for thou hast heard the words of my mouth. I will sing praise to thee in the sight of the angels"). Lauds always includes a psalm of praise, and on every solemnity, the song sung at Lauds is that of the three youths in the fiery furnace (Dn 3:56–88). This song explicitly invites the praise of the angels:

> Bless the Lord, all you works of the Lord;
> sing praise to him and highly exalt him forever.
> Bless the Lord, you heavens;
> sing praise to him and highly exalt him forever.
> Bless the Lord, you angels of the Lord;
> sing praise to him and highly exalt him forever." (vv.57–59)

Praying Lauds, then, is a practical and concrete way that we can join the angels in praise and increase our gratitude to God in imitation of them. Even if we do not have time to pray Lauds, however, we can ask for angelic support in our morning prayers. The morning, when the sun rises and reminds us of God's radiance (and so also his angels), is a natural time to be thankful, to look forward to a new day, and to see each day as a blessing that we did not earn.

Another time when the angels are said to rejoice and to give thanks to God is on the occasion of our repentance. In the parable of the Good Shepherd, Jesus tells us that he will leave ninety-nine sheep in the fold and go in search of one that is lost. This he compares to the return of those who have gone astray: "Just so, I tell you, there will be more joy in heaven over one sinner who repents than over ninety-nine righteous persons who need no repentance. . . . I tell you, there is joy in the presence of the angels of God over one sinner who repents" (Lk 15:7, 10). We can, therefore, ask for angelic encouragement to go to Confession, and we can perform our acts of penance with their help or even with the simple happy knowledge that these acts bring the angels joy. Having this angelic perspective on Penance can perhaps help to curtail dread or fear of the sacrament, and help us to thank God for the mercy offered therein, which is a source of angelic rejoicing.

In addition to gratitude, awareness of the angelic presence can increase our piety and our sense of awe. The most obvious place where our sense of awe may be deepened is at the Eucharistic liturgy. As discussed at length in chapter 4, the angels attend the liturgy and join our praise and sacrifice to their own. If we manage even some small awareness at the moment of the Sanctus that our voices are joined with the heavenly court, it will surely increase our sense of awe. The seraphim who sing this song in Isaiah 6 are seen in the vision as having six wings; with two they cover their face, with two they cover their feet, and with two they fly. This image evokes the holiness of God, such that the angels dare not uncover their faces or walk in his holy presence. In the vision, an angel also brings a coal from the heavenly altar to touch Isaiah's lips and cleanse his sins. Ephrem the Syrian uses this scripture passage to heighten our awareness of the awe-inspiring nature of the Eucharist (in the Syrian tradition, it is common to use the image of the divine coal for the Eucharist):

> [The seraph] did not hold it, and [Isaiah] did not eat it
> But to us our Lord has given both. . . .
> Fire came down and consumed the sacrifices of Elijah.
> The fire of mercy has become for us a living sacrifice.
> Fire consumed the offering:
> Your fire, O our Lord, we have eaten in your offering.
> "Who holds the wind in the palm of his hand?"
> Come see,
> O Solomon, the thing which the Lord of your father has done:
> Fire and Spirit, contrary to nature,
> Mingle and flow into the palms of his disciples!
> (*Hymns on Faith* 10, trans. Jeffrey T. Wickes)

In order to foster this sense of awe, we can listen for the parts of the liturgy that mention the angels (there are probably more than you've noticed before!). We can also read the book of Revelation (especially the visions of the heavenly liturgy in chapters 4 and 19) and meditate on the heavenly court when these passages are read on All Saints' Day. Finally, we can pray for the help of the angels in participating in the Eucharistic sacrifice in a worthy manner.

The third and perhaps most delightful disposition that can be brought about by our fellowship with angels is serenity, a sense of peace and confidence. This sense can be cultivated especially by our awareness of our guardian angel. We know, of course, that God is always present to us and dwells in our soul. But we humans who thrive on knowledge through particulars can also delight in the idea that an angel is set to watch over us and care for us. This knowledge assures us that God is not some distant watchmaker who sets the universe in motion; rather, he is concerned for each one of us "little ones" (cf. Mt 18:10). We are worth more than many sparrows, and every hair on our head is numbered (Lk 12:7). If in our weakness we falter or hesitate to do some good work for God, perhaps it will help if we can remember that an angel is there to guide us, whose created powers exceed what we can imagine. One way we can remind ourselves to trust our guardian angels and to invoke them is to say the guardian angel prayer:

Angel of God, my guardian dear,
to whom his love entrusts me here,
ever this day (or night) be at my side
to light and guard, to rule and guide.
Amen.

Moreover, the broader sense of the guardianship of the angels that we have discussed can help us in our serenity, not only about our own personal difficulties but about world events, too. If there is a guardian of every nation and every parish, then we can be sure that there is someone who cares for the events that affect our country and our Church even more deeply than we do and that they can care for these things without anxiety, fully in view of God's providence. There are many events in our lives and in the world over which we have little control, but let us not fear, knowing that the angels of God are appointed to watch and guard in ways beyond imagining.

We can cultivate these three dispositions of gratitude, piety, and serenity when we celebrate the feasts of the angels: the Feast of the Archangels on September 29 and the Feast of the Guardian Angels on October 2. Autumn has always been a time of great gratitude, as the modern holiday of Thanksgiving attests. This gratitude derives from the bounty of the harvest; it is the season when we remember that all life and sustenance is a gift from God. In addition to gratitude, the angelic feasts can increase our piety and awe by reminding us of particular instances of angelic aid in the history of salvation, naming the angels that we have come to know through scripture. Lastly, these feasts encourage us to trust in God and be at peace as we approach winter. For most of human history, winter could mean illness, starvation, or death. Although we normally do not face such fears today, nonetheless winter can seem long and joyless, and we face more darkness in nature and often in our lives. Commemorating the light of the angels and their guardianship can bring us peace as we enter into this season. For these reasons Michaelmas (i.e., the Feast of St. Michael on September 29) was long a major feast of the Western Church, a notable mark on the calendar year. It was observed with harvest feasting, and often by eating goose (comparable, perhaps, to our modern tradition of turkey at Thanksgiving). Keeping these feasts is another way we can honor the angels and increase our awareness of them.

7.

WHO ARE THE FALLEN ANGELS, AND SHOULD I FEAR THEM?

This book is primarily concerned with our heavenly helpers—the saints and the good angels—and not with our spiritual adversaries. Nevertheless, the fallen angels (who are also called demons) have come up a number of times in passing, and before we go on to discuss the saints, it is worthwhile to clarify briefly who the demons are and what their relation is to us and to the good angels.

There is no doubt that the devil and his angels exist and desire the destruction of humankind. In response to the modern tendency to psychologize or dismiss all such spiritual realities, the Congregation for the Doctrine of the Faith produced a short document in 1975 titled *Christian Faith and Demonology*, which demonstrates from scripture (such as Jesus's encounters with demons in the gospels) and tradition (particularly the Fourth Lateran Council) that the devil exists and that the Church acknowledges as real the spiritual battles that are carried on during this life. Paul speaks of this warfare quite directly: "For our struggle is not against enemies of blood and flesh, but against the rulers, against the authorities, against the cosmic powers of this present darkness, against the spiritual forces of evil in the heavenly places" (Eph 6:12).

We do not know much about the angelic fall that brought about the division of the good angels from the evil ones, only that it must have some similarity to the human fall. Just as Adam and Eve were given the chance to exercise their freedom in choosing either for or against God, so also the angels faced some similar test. Scripture alludes to this fall but does not attempt to explain the nature of it: "God did not spare the angels when they sinned, but cast them into hell and committed them to chains of deepest darkness to be kept until the judgment" (2 Pt 2:4). The *Catechism* says of this fall that it "consists in the free choice of these created spirits, who radically and irrevocably rejected God and his reign" (§392). However this choice manifested, Satan's sin (and that of the angels who fell with him) is in some way a sin of pride, of trying to set himself up as God. This desire is reflected in the way the devil tempts Adam and Eve, telling them, "You will be like God, knowing good and evil" (Gn 3:5). It is also dramatized in the book of Revelation, where the dragon and the beast are worshipped as gods (see, for example, Revelation 13:4). Why is this angelic choice irrevocable? As we have discussed already, angels do not have bodies, and therefore they do not change in the same way that we do (our bodies and our bodily experiences grow and change over time). Just as our time for wavering ends at the death of our body, so the angel's decision comes along with the acceptance of its own creaturely state. It is in an angel's nature to accept or reject once for all (knowing, as angels do, more simply through universals), where it is ours to work through particulars in time as we make decisions bit by bit.

Though fallen, these beings are still angels. They possess superior powers of mind and can exercise that power more freely because they are incorporeal. The evil angels are less powerful than the good angels, however, because sin always darkens our intellect and will, and the fallen angels do not have the power of God working directly in and through them as the good angels do. This superiority of the good angels is dramatized in scripture in the battle scene of Revelation 12, where the heavenly host led by St. Michael is victorious over the dragon and his angels: "And war broke out in heaven; Michael and his angels fought against the dragon. The dragon and his angels fought back, but they were defeated, and there was no longer any place for them in heaven" (vv. 7–8). The evil angels are free rational creatures made by God, and he allows them to be free until the Last Judgment.

Why God should permit the evil angels any power is somewhat of a mystery, but he likewise gives human beings the ability to choose against him and even to be a stumbling block to others. It is by no means self-evident, for example, why God should allow Satan to tempt and torture Job (see Job 1:6–12), although we can see that greater glory for God and wisdom for Job come through the test. Anything that the demons do on earth has been permitted by God and can be used by him to achieve his own ends. It is within the power of God to use the free choices of his own creatures for his own purposes without violating their freedom. But we should still understand that the demons are wholly under God's power and that God is not locked in some interminable dualistic conflict whose outcome is uncertain. This is evident in the fact that Christ has already conquered the demons and has authority over them; they recognize him and fear him. For example, when a man possessed by the demons known as "Legion" (meaning many, since a Roman legion is the largest of its military divisions) sees Jesus from afar, he cries out, "What have you to do with me, Jesus, Son of the Most High God? I adjure you by God, do not torment me" (Mk 5:7). This legion of demons then begs to be cast into nearby pigs. This plea demonstrates that the demons do not even attempt to do battle directly with Jesus, knowing that Jesus can do whatever he wills with them.

What, then, do the devil and his angels want from us? Why do they tempt us? In all of the various kinds of trials that happen in our lives (whether through the influence of demons or not), there is really only one temptation. Job's wife puts it to Job rather starkly: "Do you still persist in your integrity? Curse God, and die" (Jb 2:9). The demons want us to renounce God and thereby perish. They want us to turn away from God—to stop trusting him, to stop obeying him, and to stop worshipping him. This temptation can happen in very obvious ways, like that of the lure of idolatry and the worship of false gods in the Old Testament. It is for a good reason that the first commandment is to worship God alone; the perennial sin of the Israelites was to turn away from that worship. But this temptation to idolatry can happen in much more subtle ways, such as putting money, career, or politics over God. In short, the devil will be happy for us to look at anything—including (perhaps most dangerously) ourselves and our own accomplishments—so long as he can convince us to look away from God.

This self-turning behavior is the sin of pride out of which the devil fell, and he would have us follow his course. In one of the most famous passages from *City of God*, Augustine explains this idea by describing the city of God (in which the angels dwell), and the city of man (in which demons dwell) as two cities defined by love:

> Two loves, then, have made two cities. Love of self, even to the point of contempt for God, made the earthly city, and love of God, even to the point of contempt for self, made the heavenly city. Thus the former glories in itself, and the latter glories in the Lord. The former seeks its glory from men, but

> the latter finds its highest glory in God, the witness of our conscience. . . . The former loves its own strength, displayed in its men of power; the latter says to its God, *I love you, O Lord, my strength* (Ps 18:1). (*City of God* 14.28, trans. William Babcock)

Life, then, it would appear, is one long temptation, one long struggle in which the enemy is ever vigilant. Peter warns us of this: "Discipline yourselves, keep alert. Like a roaring lion your adversary the devil prowls around, looking for someone to devour" (1 Pt 5:8). But should this state of affairs mean that we ought to *fear* the demons? Perhaps the best response to this question is found in the words of Paul: "If God is for us, who is against us? He who did not withhold his own Son, but gave him up for all of us, will he not with him also give us everything else?" (Rom 8:31–32). The demons obey Christ's every word, and even his disciples were given power over unclean spirits (see Mark 6:7; Matthew 10:1). Although being aware of this spiritual dimension of our struggle against sin can certainly be helpful, we need not fear anyone but God alone. Think of this: if you are laboring to meet a deadline at work, would you say that you are *afraid* of the distractions at the office? Surely not. What you fear is disappointing your boss or your coworkers (or maybe losing your job). However, knowing the nature of the distractions that are most difficult for you to overcome will help ensure that you keep your timeline.

Let us not be ignorant of the demons and the ploys they might use to keep us away from God, and let us not underestimate their ability to assess and exploit our weaknesses. But let us not fear them. Let us not seek out knowledge of them other than what is given in scripture, because this is even more likely to lead to superstition or error than in the case of the good angels. Let us rather trust in God and be assured also of the help of his angels, who are just as near to us as are their fallen brethren, but who are more powerful and secure.

PART II
SAINTS

8.

WHAT IS A SAINT, AND AM I BECOMING ONE?

Hopefully we now have a clearer picture of our angelic brethren, those celestial spirits who help and guide us and with whom we will praise the Lord forever in the heavenly city. But what about other human beings who have died before us in the peace of Christ and are now seeing God face-to-face? Are they the ones whom we call "saints"? Do they help us? And if they are merely human, why should we pray to them? In the second half of this book we will address these and similar questions.

The very first question—what is a saint?—turns out to have a more complex answer than one might first expect. The word "saint" comes from the Latin word *sanctus*, which means "holy." This is a word we encountered when speaking of the threefold hymn of the seraphim in chapter 4. When Paul writes to the various churches, he sometimes uses a similar address, writing to all of the "holy ones" (in Greek, *hagioi*) in a particular place, and in many translations this word is simply rendered as "saints." For example, the opening of the letter of Paul to the Philippians reads: "Paul and Timothy, servants of Christ Jesus, To all the saints in Christ Jesus who are in Philippi, with the bishops and deacons: Grace to you and peace from God our Father and the Lord Jesus Christ" (1:1–2). To be called a "saint," then, means to be saintly, to be holy; these two words are synonyms. But what is holiness?

Holiness is difficult to define. When we apply the word to human beings, we might think of someone who is good, who lives a virtuous life. When we apply it to the angels, we might think of a being that is radiant and close to God—we might even think of it as something that is a bit scary. When we apply it to objects (like the holy vessels on the altar or the Holy Bible), we might think of something that is sacred. One definition that encompasses all of these ideas is "set apart for a sacred purpose." But God himself is perfectly holy (in fact, the only one to whom the word fully applies), and he does not merely serve some sacred purpose, although he is set apart in the sense of being utterly transcendent. So another good way to think of holiness is as having a likeness to God. And how do you become like God? You participate in God's own life. This participation happens primarily by worship, by partaking of God's glory in giving yourself to him.

This understanding of holiness as a doxological category (a category pertaining to glory) explains all of our different articulations of holiness. An object—like a golden chalice used at Mass—is holy because it participates in worship of God insofar as it can as an inanimate thing, and it has been blessed for this purpose. A human being worships God by being a living sacrifice; this entails the struggle against sin and the attempt to live more and more according to the commandments, especially the commandment to love God and our neighbor as ourselves. This path to holiness also, of course, entails specific and embodied acts of worship, especially in the sacraments. The sacraments are the mode of worship that is particular to us as creatures with both body and soul. An angel is already holy because its whole life is an act of praise and worship; an angel participates in God's life in a very high degree (which also explains an angel's tendency to overawe people!).

When we understand that holiness is a word that denotes something about our relationship to God as creatures who worship him, it is easier to see why the word is used in such a broad manner. When speaking of holiness as it applies to human beings, we can imagine concentric circles of holiness, as we draw ever nearer to God himself. (See the illustration on the next page.)

The largest circle indicates that of the baptized. When we are baptized, our soul receives an indelible character that sets us apart for worship of God and designates us as a member of Christ's Church. For this reason, we can call all baptized Christians saints, as Paul does when he addresses all the faithful at a particular church. To be holy in a greater degree is to practice the faith—to worship God in his Church and to live

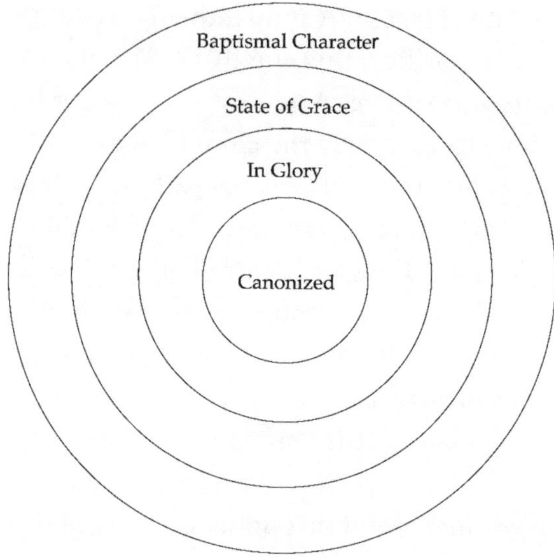

a life that is free from mortal sin. A person who lives such a life is said to be in a state of grace and is on the way to the heavenly homeland. Those who persist in their worship and die in a state of grace will arrive in the beatific vision, where they will be invited into the life of the Blessed Trinity and worship God without end. These people are holy in a secure way and are said to be in glory.

Of those who are in glory, there is a further group of canonized saints. These are people whom the Church on earth publicly *recognizes* as being in glory. This last group is the one that we Catholics normally associate with the word "saint" and will be the subject of chapter 10. Regarding these saints, here it suffices to say that even the category of canonized saint is one that pertains to worship. Canonized saints, of course, do not necessarily worship God better or more fully than the unknown saints in glory. Nevertheless, their lives and examples become part of *our* worship; canonized saints are invoked in the Mass, they are celebrated in the Church's liturgical calendar, and they are honored in the individual lives of many Catholics who develop devotions to particular saints.

So, are *you* a saint? If you are a baptized Christian, there is a real sense in which you can be called a saint; that is, you can be called holy. You are marked with the indelible baptismal seal of Christ. Are you *becoming* a saint? If you are living your life so as to worship God, persisting in a state of grace, then you are becoming holier, becoming more saintly, so to speak, as you travel toward the heavenly Jerusalem. It is there that we will finally be saints, properly speaking. After being purified of all sin, we will, like the seraphim, be aflame in our praise of God, in unity with the Holy Trinity.

This dual reality (that we are holy but also becoming holy; that we are saints but also becoming saints) is part of the Apostles' Creed, as we say that we believe in "the holy catholic Church." In this article of faith, we are professing that the Church is objectively holy—it is a people called by God to belong to himself; it is set apart. In fact, the word for "church" in both Latin and Greek (*ecclesia/ekklesia*) comes from the Greek verb *kaleo*, which means "to call." The Church is also the mystical Body of Jesus Christ, who is perfectly holy. So the Church is objectively holy. But we all know that there are many people in the Church who are not perfectly holy, or perhaps not very holy at all. So when we profess that the Church is holy, we are drawing on the whole breadth of the meaning of that word: it is objectively holy (founded by God and united to him) but also becoming more holy (in us, its members), and it is an agent of making us holier (through its whole life, and especially through the sacraments). Put otherwise, the Church is made of saints (the baptized), it makes saints (by being the agent of holiness in the world), and it declares people to be saints (by canonization).

By saying that we are becoming saints, we do not mean that we are all aiming to become canonized saints, that we are striving for public recognition of our holiness. In fact, having such a desire is a pretty good indication that we are not yet very holy. Any proper desire for recognition would have as its end only worship of God and the building up of the faithful. For this reason, many canonized saints in their own lifetime were extremely reluctant to be called saints at all, meaning that they had a very good view of themselves as creatures before God rather than as illustrious men and women in the eyes of the world. Servant of God Dorothy Day is often quoted as saying: "Don't call me a saint. I don't want to be dismissed so easily" (there is a movie about Day that bears this title). By this she indicates that the only kind of recognition she wants is one that calls other people to action—she feared that canonization would make people dismiss her example as too difficult to follow. She expresses the very sentiment that all are called to be saints whether or not they are named a saint by the Church.

So, although it might at first seem confusing that the word "saint" can be applied to all Christians, while also being used to describe particularly virtuous Christians and acting as a specific designation for canonized saints, all these uses make sense when you understand that "saint" is a word referring to holiness, and our holiness changes and grows. Having this nuanced understanding of the word "saint" will also help to clarify why we confess belief in the communion of saints. To this subject we will turn in our next chapter.

9. WHAT IS THE COMMUNION OF SAINTS?

The fact that the Church is in a sense objectively holy and made up of saints—that is, baptized people—helps to explain the meaning of the phrase "communion of saints," which comes directly after "the holy catholic Church" in the Apostles' Creed. This phrase does not primarily refer to a belief in canonized saints or their veneration. What it means is that the Church actually makes us saints by our baptism and that we have true communion with one another—the phrase is essentially a synonym for the Church. The *Catechism of the Catholic Church* says: "After confessing 'the holy catholic Church,' the Apostles' Creed adds 'the communion of saints.' In a certain sense this article is a further explanation of the preceding: 'What is the Church if not the assembly of all the saints?' The communion of saints is the Church" (§946).

If the phrase "communion of saints" essentially means the Church, we might well ask, what is the Church? It is vital to answer this question in order to understand all of the other practices of the Church pertaining to the saints. Is the Church just a group of people who like Jesus and hang out with one another? In other words, is the Church a club of baptized people? To think of the Church as a club is to misunderstand its very nature. The Church is the people of God and the Body of Christ. Let us look briefly at these two descriptions before turning to the clarification about the Church offered by the phrase "communion of saints."

The Church is the people of God. What this name means is that the will binding this people together is not primarily the will of the people but the will of God, who calls them and loves them. God has always had a people in history, a real identifiable one whom he claims as his own: "They shall be my people, and I will be their God" (Jer 32:38). The *Catechism* says that this people of God "is marked by characteristics that clearly distinguish it from all other religious, ethnic, political, or cultural groups found in history" (§782). Why? Because the Church cannot be claimed by any one person or group, its law is love, its mission is universal salvation, and its destiny is eternal. There is no club that could have anything like these characteristics, and the people of God can only make these statements about itself because of its union with God—because it is the mystical Body of Christ.

The "mystical Body of Christ" is a phrase that we have already used in passing. The reason why God became man in

Jesus Christ in the first place was to unite our humanity with his divinity, having cleansed us of all sin. He accomplishes this union in the Incarnation, in the Church, and in the Eucharist (we use the phrase "the Body of Christ" to refer to all three of these mysteries). To put it simply: God and man are brought together in the Body of Christ. So the Church is instituted by Christ on the Cross, when water and blood flow from his side (see John 19:34), indicating how we are invited to join with him in his Passion—through Baptism (water) and Eucharist (blood). Just as Adam's bride was taken from his side (Eve from Adam's rib in Genesis 2:21), so also Christ's bride, the Church, is taken from his side on the Cross and he makes us to be one flesh with him. We are therefore truly incorporated into Christ's body by the Sacraments of Initiation, as Paul explains in 1 Corinthians 12:12–13: "For just as the body is one and has many members, and all the members of the body, though many, are one body, so it is with Christ. For in the one Spirit we were all baptized into one body—Jews or Greeks, slaves or free—and we were all made to drink of one Spirit." Of the Eucharist, Christ says even more strongly: "Very truly, I tell you, unless you eat the flesh of the Son of Man and drink his blood, you have no life in you" (Jn 6:53). We say, then, that we do not make the Church by our own will; rather, Baptism and Eucharist *make* the Church. The Church is the Body of Christ, and the way that the body grows and is built up is by the ingrafting of people into that body through water and blood.

We should not think of Paul's language about the Church as body as merely metaphorical. Otherwise, calling the Church one, holy, catholic, and apostolic would be merely poetic or aspirational language, and not absolutely true. The unity Christ wills to have with his body is an intimate one, as intimate as the unity of our own bodies, as the one we experience with our own cells and limbs. Christ indicates his relationship with his mystical body when he cries out to Saul on the road to Damascus: "Saul, Saul, why do you persecute me?" (Acts 9:4). Christ does not ask, "Why do you persecute Christians?" or "Why do you persecute my Church?" but "Why do you persecute *me*?" Likewise, at the Final Judgment speech in Matthew, Christ identifies himself absolutely with his body:

> "I was naked and you gave me clothing, I was sick and you took care of me, I was in prison and you visited me." Then the righteous will answer him, "Lord, when was it that we saw you hungry and gave you food, or thirsty and gave you something to drink? And when was it that we saw you a stranger and welcomed you, or naked and gave you clothing? And when was it that we saw you sick or in prison and visited you?" And the king will answer them, "Truly I tell you, just as you did it to one of the least of these who are members of my family, you did it to me." (Mt 25:36–40)

The Church is more of an organism than an organization, and the head of that organism is Christ. Therefore, sometimes the Church is referred to as the *totus Christus*, meaning "the whole Christ," both the head (Christ in his divinity) and the body (his humanity, into which we are incorporated, and so the Church).

So the Church is not a club, but a reality both historical and mystical, founded by God himself. But we should not think that we play no role and do not respond or receive this great gift of the Church. So also, the Church is properly called the "communion of saints." "Saints" in this context refers to all the baptized; all who are part of Christ's body are saints, and they are saints because they are part of his body, and yet they are still being healed in the body and becoming holier. Although the Church is a reality brought about by God, it is a communion of free human people. It has a plural dimension (the "saints") as well as a unified or singular dimension (the "body"). We do not become one undifferentiated mass by coming into Christ's body but remain ourselves with our own unique talents, personalities, and callings. In fact, that differentiation is Paul's main point in 1 Corinthians 12—that some are eyes, others are feet, others the tongue, but all are parts of the body who need one another, and no one should look down on another. As Paul puts it: "If the whole body were an eye, where would the hearing be? . . . But as it is, God arranged the members in the body, each one of them, as he chose" (1 Cor 12:17–18).

The phrase "communion of saints" to describe the Church also clarifies that we have true contact and unity (i.e., communion) with all members of the Church, alive or dead (celestial or terrestrial). It expresses that the Church accomplishes a three-dimensional unity—vertically, between us and God; horizontally, between us and all others in God; and also backward and forward, we might say, across time and space. The phrase makes concrete the mystical unity that we all share—because the word "communion" implies sharing. What is it a sharing of? In short, everything: charisms and talents, prayer and worship, charity and love, material goods. Where a club is based on shared interest, or "communion," in a hobby (say bowling or science fiction), the Church is truly united, not by some external interest, but because we belong fully to each other. As Acts says of the first Christian community, "everything they owned was held in common" (Acts 4:32). Understanding this true unity that is the Church makes practices like tithing (giving a portion of your income to the Church) and giving to the poor quite obvious—we are one body, a communion, and would you not want to come to the aid of your own hand, your own brother? So Acts goes on to say of the Christian community, "There was not a needy person among them" (Acts 4:34).

If "saints" is a kind of generic term that covers all Christians, and all these Christians have a *de facto* communion, then why is it that the Church bothers to canonize saints and use the word in such a specific way? If all Christians are saints and there are many in glory who are not formally recognized, what is the benefit of singling out particular examples of holiness for veneration? To this topic we will now turn.

10.

WHAT IS CANONIZATION, AND WHY DOES THE CHURCH CANONIZE CERTAIN PEOPLE?

Although, as we have learned, the word "saint" can be used quite broadly, Catholics tend to reserve the word for use as a title (as in St. Joseph). In other words, we generally use the word "saint" to refer to canonized saints who are formally recognized by the Church. How does a person become formally recognized as a saint, and why does it matter?

The canonization process as we know it today is a modern phenomenon. In the ancient and medieval Church, a person who was recognized as living a holy life was often referred to in writings and memorials simply as the "holy so-and-so," for example, the holy (*sanctus*) bishop Ambrose or the holy (*sanctus*) father Benedict. The veneration of holy persons by those who knew them often led to their lives being written down and miracles being attributed to them (either while the saint was alive or through their intercession after death). Thus, the saints' cults would grow, and their bodies and memories would be venerated. Their names might even be mentioned in the liturgy or their stories read at church. That is, in fact, why we refer to certain saints as "canonized," meaning they belong to a "canon"—an authorized list for the purposes of worship, like the canon of scripture. One of the earliest attestations of the veneration of the body of a saint comes from *Martyrdom of Polycarp*, which was likely written in the third century but draws on earlier memories of the martyr, who died around the year 155. "We afterwards took up his bones, more precious than costly stones and more excellent than gold, and interred them in a decent place. There the Lord will permit us, as far as possible, to assemble in rapturous joy and celebrate his martyrdom—his birthday—both in order to commemorate the heroes that have gone before, and to train and prepare the heroes yet to come" (*Martyrdom of Polycarp* 18.2–3, trans. James A. Kleist).

Saintly devotions are very ancient, therefore, but some had more historical and theological bases than others. Sometimes the zeal for the veneration of the saints and the love of a good saint story led to less-than-accurate portrayals of their lives. Such practices and hagiographies (holy biographies) came under attack during the Reformation. This criticism led to a more formal process of canonization and a more thorough investigation into the saints' lives and the miracles attributed to them, although even prior to the Reformation the pope was canonizing saints. This magisterial recognition came along with the desire for greater legitimization of a saint's cult. The modern process of canonization with which we are familiar, however, began with Pope Benedict XIV (pope from 1740 to 1758) and was most recently revised by Pope John Paul II in the 1980s.

Today, a person is declared a saint through the following process. First, a diocesan bishop must ask permission to open the cause for canonization. Usually, a waiting period of five years after the death of the holy person is imposed in order to allow the deeds of that person's life to come to light and to see the lasting effect of his or her sanctity, although this waiting period can be waived in exceptional circumstances (as it was most recently for John Paul II and Mother Teresa). If there is no objection, the cause is opened and the person is named "Servant of God." Then information is gathered regarding the life and virtues of the person. Much like the informal canonization process of ages past, it is among those who knew the person and those who were affected most immediately by his or her life that the veneration must begin.

After all of the testimonies and data are collected concerning the Servant of God (called the *acta*), they are submitted to the Dicastery for the Causes of Saints (formerly the Congregation for the Causes of Saints) at the Vatican. A person appointed by the dicastery collates and summarizes the information, which is then voted upon by the dicastery's members. The dicastery considers whether the Servant displayed heroic virtue—whether he or she exercised faith, hope, charity, prudence, justice, fortitude, and temperance in a high degree. Other traditional marks of sanctity, such as habits of prayer and frequenting of the sacraments, are also considered.

If the vote is in the affirmative, it is passed on to the pope for a final decision. If the pope confirms the vote, the Servant of God is declared "Venerable." In order to be promoted to the rank of "Blessed" (what we would consider a formally canonized saint who is eligible for public veneration), the Venerable must have a verified miracle attributed to his or her intercession. One who is Blessed can then be incorporated into the public worship of the diocese that promoted the cause and/or other "local" communities (for example, a religious community of whom the saint was a part). In practice, however, a Blessed can receive veneration almost anywhere, especially as saints are much more globally accessible today than in the past. In order to be considered fully canonized, however, and eligible for the public veneration of the universal Church, a second miracle must be attributed to the saint's intercession. Of course, when an individual is declared a saint, the pope does not *make* a saint, strictly speaking; rather, he authoritatively affirms their place among those in glory. We also must remember that these steps pertain to authorizing the *public* veneration of a particular person, and there is much more latitude for veneration in our private devotions.

Why is a miracle the litmus test for canonization? Miracle working would seem to fall under suspicion today. But a miracle is seen as a sign of God's approval that a particular individual should be incorporated into the Church's life of worship (remembering that holiness is a doxological category). God is allowing the saint a share in his glory and so to be involved in his own worship in a special way. It also stands to reason that one who is in glory can intercede in this definitive way to aid those on earth, and so it is a kind of visible confirmation of their invisible spiritual state. Lastly, in the ancient church, holy persons were often involved in miracle working (as was Jesus himself, who produced many signs), and so it is a traditional sign of sanctity. We must also remember that it is not miracles alone that affirm the sanctity of a particular individual, but all of the evidence and testimony of their virtue presented in the first phase of canonization. All of this means that formal canonization is a high bar, and for good reason, since the Church is setting up this individual for imitation and as an intercessor.

This whole system seems rather complex, however, even when boiled down, and the process can take years and years. Why bother with it? First, it is good to note that veneration and imitation of holy lives has always been a part of the Church's life, long before a formalized process was established. Formal canonization is an organic development in the Church's life of worship, more needed as the Church grew and then entered into skeptical modernity. There are also many benefits to having formal approval of a particular person's life of holiness, and here we will discuss a few.

One of the first benefits of formal canonization is making the reality of heaven tangible. Rather than having a generic notion that people who die in friendship with God will go to heaven, we have specific, concrete examples of people who have done just that. Moreover, not only can we name people in the beatific vision, but we can also *act* on this belief by asking these saints to pray for us. It is one thing to say that we believe in life after death, but it is another to enact this belief and speak with the dead. We do not merely have a hazy concept of loved ones "looking down," but we believe that we can commune with them by praying to them, invoking them in the liturgy, and being united to them in the Eucharist. In short, that the Church canonizes saints is the surest sign of our belief in "life everlasting," as we confess in the Creed.

Second, canonized saints give us authorized models for imitation. As human beings, we love to make idols of our heroes—whether sports stars or actors or even politicians. But most of the people who are powerful and famous in this life are not worthy of our wholehearted admiration and certainly should not be imitated in every aspect of their lives. With the saints, it is a different story. The lives of the saints have been thoroughly examined and approved by the highest authority of the Church (the pope) and the authority of heaven (through miracles). We can have confidence in reading about the saints and following their example. All Christians follow the example of Christ, of course, but the saints are like little Christs, imitating him in different times and places so that we can have a picture of Christlikeness throughout history. Christ, after all, was not a mother, he was not an American, he was not a lawyer—but there are saints who were, and they help us see what Christ's life looks like in many different circumstances. St. Paul urges the Philippians, "Brothers and sisters, join in imitating me, and observe those who live according to the example you have in us" (3:17). Following Paul, who invites others to imitate his life, we imitate those who have lived an exemplary life in Christ. In his homily for the canonization Mass of ten new saints in May 2022, Pope Francis said that "a saint is a luminous reflection of the Lord of history." In other words, the lives of the saints are like a prism, refracting the pure white light of Christ into many different colors so that we can see him in different ways, a kind of spectrum of Christ's beauty. In the lives of the saints, we can see Christ's life reflected and so draw closer to him.

The Church's invitation to imitate the saints in their exemplary way of life is not a mere accommodation to human weakness, as if the truly strong would just follow Christ's image alone and unaided. Rather, the incorporation of the saints into Christ's life is a part of God's plan. The Church, as discussed in chapter 9, is the mystical Body of Christ; it truly becomes him and represents him on earth. Christ did not ascend into heaven and drop the Bible out of the sky as a how-to guide, leaving us to get on with the job of coming after him. Rather, he promised, "I am with you always, to the end of the age" (Mt 28:20). Christ is with us by the indwelling of the Holy Spirit and in the sacraments; that is, he is present in his body, the Church, which the Holy Spirit animates and which dispenses his sacraments. This activity is not accidental or extra, but part of Christ's plan to bring all humanity to himself and unite them in himself. Christ's life is continually lived and re-presented in his saints.

A third benefit of having formally canonized saints is the hope and confidence we experience as we see that heaven and holiness are attainable by every kind of person. No matter what your state in life—married, single, vowed religious, or widowed—you can find a saint who is like you. No matter what time period or place you live in, you can find a saint who has walked a similar path and faced similar trials. No matter what point in your life you started to practice your faith, you can find a saint who did likewise. No matter who you are and what difficulties you face, because of canonized saints, you can have absolute confidence that God is able to make you holy and bring you to himself.

The lives of the saints are the essential visible sign of the Church's holiness. As we have already discussed, it is an article of faith to profess that the Church is holy. Yet, there are necessarily visible signs of this spiritual reality; otherwise it would be an offense to our reason to believe it. There is plenty of sinfulness in the Church, and it would be nearly impossible to believe that her holiness is founded on and vouchsafed by Christ without his saints. In these truly heroic lives, we can glimpse what God is really doing in the world and in his Church.

Some people might be satisfied to view the saints solely as holy exemplars and encouragements on our journey. In fact, chapter 11 of Hebrews sets up the patriarchs and many Old Testament figures as just those kinds of models and describes their lives as an exhortation to us. But as we have already mentioned in this chapter, Catholics also believe that the saints are intercessors—that we can ask for their prayers. The reason behind this practice and its fruits will be the subject of the next chapter.

11.

WHY WOULD I EVER PRAY TO A SAINT IF I CAN JUST PRAY TO GOD?

In the previous chapter, we mentioned that the saints are invoked in the liturgy; we ask for their intercession, and we confess and worship in their presence (for example, in the Confiteor said at the beginning of Mass). What does it mean to ask for the intercession of a saint, and what is the point of it, if we can just pray directly to God? Isn't there only "one mediator between God and humankind, Christ Jesus, himself human" (1 Tm 2:5)? Sometimes the Catholic Church is accused of heaping up mediators between ourselves and God, like a stack of dominoes.

When we pray to a saint, first of all, we are not asking for the saint to accomplish some work apart from or instead of God. We speak of praying to a saint as a shorthand; it means that we ask for the saint's intercession. In other words, we ask for the saint to pray to God for us. This request is a natural extension of our understanding that we have real communion with the dead and can speak to them. Just as we would ask our friends on earth to pray for us in a time of difficulty, so we can turn to our heavenly friends and ask them to pray for us. And why is it that our fellow Christians are able to pray to God for us? It is because they have a relationship both with God and with us, and it is normal for families to talk to one another about one another, to care for one another, to keep one another in their minds and hearts. We would think it silly to insist that each individual person talk to God only about themselves; in fact, that would be quite unhealthy. We are commanded to love both God and our neighbor (see Mark 12:30–31; Matthew 22:37–39; Luke 10:27), and for our own good.

It follows, then, that the saints are the perfect people to ask for prayers, since they are part of our spiritual family and are closer to God than anyone else we know. They are also in an even better position to petition than our friends here on earth, because they no longer have any need to worry or to pray for their own concerns—their love for God and neighbor are operating in perfect harmony. They have no distractions in prayer, nor do they forget our requests. But we should not think of the mediation of a saint as anything other than the mediation of Christ. If the Church is the mystical Body of Christ, we can understand that saints are perfectly incorporated into that body in heaven; they are Christ's hands, his feet, and his eyes. If some friends were to lift a heavy box for us, we would not claim that their hands, rather than that they themselves, had done the lifting. So also when Christ's hands—his saints—do some heavy lifting in our lives, we count it as nothing other than the work of Christ.

So perhaps now we can see that the saints' intercession is not in competition with Christ's, but is of a piece with it. But still, we might wonder why we would choose to have recourse to a saint rather than just pray to Christ directly. If the saint only works by Christ's power anyway, isn't saintly intercession second-rate or derivative? To think in this way, however, is to miss entirely what God wants to accomplish in Christ and what it means to be in Christ's body. Being in Christ's body not only means to be united to God—because Christ is God, although it certainly does mean that—it also means to be united to one another perfectly. Is this not what the human heart desires? Not only to be with God, but also to love everyone as we ought—to understand them, to live in peace and fellowship with them? The story of human history is one of love and longing for unity—and of trying to gain that love or unity by force. But Christ gained that perfect unity on the Cross, not by force, but by laying down his life for his friends. In other words, he died that we might be his friend and be friends with one another. There is no greater compliment to Christ's sacrifice than that we love each other in him; in fact, he commands us to do so: "By this everyone will know that you are my disciples, if you have love for one another" (Jn 13:35).

Let us consider an analogy. Let's say that you have been dating someone for a few months and are beginning to have a serious relationship. Your boyfriend (or girlfriend) then asks you to come home with him to meet his parents. Would you respond: "Why would I ever want to meet your parents? I only want to spend time with you!" This response would be considered bizarre and also hurtful. To fully love and understand your boyfriend, it is natural to meet his friends and his family. And if you make your boyfriend's family into your own and take his friends as your friends, then your love is all the stronger and happier for it. The saints are the friends of God. Christ tells his disciples before his Passion: "I do not call you servants any longer, because the servant does not know what the master is doing; but I have called you friends, because I have made known to you everything that I have heard from my Father" (Jn 15:15). The saints likewise see God face-to-face and know everything the Father has to reveal. By spending time in the saints' company through prayer or spiritual reading, you come to know Christ better and to love him more strongly.

This teaching of the Church on the saints is not, then, some capitulation to popular piety, a concession to the masses who need their earthly heroes. It is in fact very beautiful and a foretaste of heaven. When God's love is embraced to the full, it encompasses all things, including all of humanity. This teaching on the intercession of the saints means that the beatific vision is not a monotonous contemplation of a divine monad. Rather, it is, as Paul describes it, when God will be all in all (see 1 Corinthians 15:28; Ephesians 1:23). Our relationship with each other (the communion of saints) will be perfected in heaven, and so it will also be communion with God himself. Conversely, communion with God himself will not take away from or compete with our love for other people, for we will all be like God and participate in his life together. This vision of heaven is completely consonant with our understanding that God himself is Trinity, a communion of persons—Father, Son, and Holy Spirit—who live a life of eternal love and self-gift.

So, then, we can go even further in understanding how the intercession of the saints is a fulfillment of God's plan, because God does not wish to unite us in himself as one undifferentiated lump. He wants to free us to be most fully ourselves, the people whom he created us to be, and part of being human means exercising our free will and cooperating in God's plan. Miracles worked through the intercession of the saints or prayers answered with their aid allow precisely for this cooperation. When we reach the beatific vision, we become fully united in God's saving plan, truly and freely participating in his acts of love. St. Thomas Aquinas offers a wonderful analogy for how this participation works. He imagines a workshop, where the master has perfected his trade and has also trained up many apprentices in his art who are capable of working with him and for him. Such a master takes great pleasure when he sees that his apprentices are capable of doing what he has done and that his customers might go to the apprentice just as they would come to him. In a similar way, parents are proud when their children care for one another. So also God wants to work for us and in us and through us, and he takes delight that we can come to his apprentices, his children, the saints. He will take even more delight when we too become his apprentices and work with him.

Lastly, and most practically, the saints are a great comfort in the Christian life. Even if we have a very strong trust in God and love for him, there are still many consolations offered to us by our friends and family in this earthly life that is so full of sorrows and cares. The saints are just like those friends, but they are always faithful, they are always ready to listen, and they never make inappropriate demands of us. Anyone who has taken time to read the lives of the saints and some of their writings is sure to find a kindred spirit among them, someone who speaks to their heart and to their life's experience. What's more is that when we make friends with the saints, we can in turn strengthen our friendships with our Christian brethren here on earth, because many of them have devotions to the same saints. The saints are like those friends we have who are always throwing parties, making connections, and bringing people together. And unlike a worldly hero or idol whom we can only admire from a distance, a saint wants to be called our friend, just as Christ does. The saints make themselves available to us; they want to help us and to bring us finally to that heavenly homeland where they await us.

As with the angels, a special moment of unity with the saints in prayer is during the Eucharistic liturgy. It is here where we ask for the saints' intercession as a community. The intercessions take place after the Eucharist has been consecrated, near the end of the Eucharistic prayer. Sometimes it is simple, naming a few saints such as Mary and Joseph. If the prayer of the Roman Canon is used, it will have a long list of saints' names, including many early Christian martyrs, bishops, and popes. That prayer begins like this: "To us, also, your servants, who, though sinners, hope in your abundant mercies, graciously grant some share and fellowship with your holy Apostles and Martyrs: with John the Baptist, Stephen, Matthias . . ." Note that the prayer is not being made directly to these saints, but rather it is a prayer for communion with them through the sharing of the Eucharist. Given our discussion above, we can see that this prayer is very fitting. The Eucharist is the Body of Christ, not only the true presence of his body, blood, soul, and divinity, but also the presence of his whole mystical body. As Augustine explains:

> So if you want to understand the body of Christ, listen to the apostle telling the faithful, *You,*

> *though, are the body of Christ and its members* (1 Cor 12:27). So if it's you that are the body of Christ and its members, it's the mystery meaning you that has been placed on the Lord's table; what you receive is the mystery that means you. It is to what you are that you reply *Amen*, and by so replying you express your assent. What you hear, you see, is *The body of Christ*, and you answer, *Amen*. So be a member of the body of Christ, in order to make that *Amen* true. (*Sermon* 272, trans. Edmund Hill; italics mine)

By saying that the Eucharist is the "mystery meaning you," Augustine means to express that in the Eucharist we receive our own true selves, because we are meant for unity with God and his saints. We present ourselves on the altar in unity with Christ to become a living sacrifice. In this way, we effect the unity of the Church and are in communion with the saints.

So why do we pray to the saints? For the same reason we talk to our Christian brothers and sisters here on earth, and for the same reason that we support each other and love each other. We are united to the saints as we are to all Christians, especially in the Mass, where we are likewise united in a special way to those physically present at Mass. But the saints can be even better friends to us than those here, because they are perfected in charity and are sitting now in God's presence. Let us not hesitate to turn to them and spend time with them in God's company, to be united with them in one body.

12.
WHAT ARE RELICS, AND WHY DO CATHOLICS VENERATE THEM?

The word "relic" comes from the Latin word *reliqua*, and it means something that is left behind. In other words, relics are the remains of the saints (this includes things left behind by Christ himself, such as the relics of the true Cross). Primarily, the word "relic" refers to the body or part of the body of a saint (what is known today as a "first-class relic"), but it can also refer to other remains, such as a saint's clothing or items that he or she has used (a "second-class relic"). We even recognize what are called "third-class relics"—objects that have been put into contact with a first-class relic. But where does the practice of venerating a saint's body come from, and what does it mean?

First, there are biblical examples of the bones of the saints or objects belonging to them having wonder-working power. In the Old Testament, the bones of the prophet Elisha bring a man back to life: "So Elisha died, and they buried him. Now bands of Moabites used to invade the land in the spring of the year. As a man was being buried, a marauding band was seen and the man was thrown into the grave of Elisha; as soon as the man touched the bones of Elisha, he came to life and stood on his feet" (2 Kgs 13:20–21). We also have a New Testament example in the book of Acts, where "relics" of the apostle Paul effect healings: "God did extraordinary miracles through Paul, so that when the handkerchiefs or aprons that had touched his skin were brought to the sick, their diseases left them, and the evil spirits came out of them" (Acts 19:11–12).

Unsurprisingly, then, the Christian practice of visiting and honoring the bodies of the saints and celebrating the Eucharist at their tombs is very ancient. We already saw a passage from *Martyrdom of Polycarp* relating that the bones of Polycarp were gathered and that they were visited on the day of the martyr's death (his "birthday" into heaven) and honored. It is also witnessed by Tertullian, who lived from the second to the third centuries in North Africa. In a similar vein, the place where the early martyr-bishop Cyprian died (d. 258) was known by the name *mensa Cypriani*, the table or altar of Cyprian, because of the celebrations that took place there on the martyr's death date.

Going out to the tombs of the beloved dead might seem like an obvious practice, and visiting gravesites to make an offering is certainly something cross-cultural, not unique to early Christianity. Christians, however, took this veneration a step further by bringing the bodies of the saints *into* churches, a practice that is first noted in the fourth century. This action was peculiar to Christians—pagans would have thought it unwise and bizarre to bring the dead among the living. Much like today, death was kept at the edges of society and out of sight. One of the most famous patristic examples of the translation of relics comes from Ambrose of Milan, who discovered the bodies of the martyrs Protasius and Gervasius and placed them under the altar of the church in Milan. This moment made an impression on the younger Augustine of Hippo, who writes about it in his *Confessions*, recounting miracles that occurred during the procession of the relics to the basilica (see *Confessions* 9.7.16). The procession of bones into a city is an inversion of the social order. Rather than a triumphant emperor returning from battle, the dead march in triumph, having despoiled no lesser enemy than death himself. Fittingly, then, the saint's bones are sources of healing power, overcoming death in a minor way in the lives of the faithful.

The rationale for wanting to put a holy person's bones in a place of honor and venerate them is already hinted at in the subversive nature of the practice. Where the heroes of this world die and have power no longer, Christian heroes are believed to be alive in heaven. And more than that, Christians profess faith in the resurrection of the dead—that all people at the end of time will rise to receive their bodies again at the

Last Judgment. Paul describes this moment beautifully in 1 Corinthians:

> Listen, I will tell you a mystery! We will not all die, but we will all be changed, in a moment, in the twinkling of an eye, at the last trumpet. For the trumpet will sound, and the dead will be raised imperishable, and we will be changed. For this perishable body must put on imperishability, and this mortal body must put on immortality. When this perishable body puts on imperishability, and this mortal body puts on immortality, then the saying that is written will be fulfilled: "Death has been swallowed up in victory." "Where, O death, is your victory? Where, O death, is your sting?" (15:51–55)

The link between Christ's defeat of death, which he shares with all humanity in the Resurrection, and the veneration of relics in the early church is especially obvious because all of the earliest saints venerated in this way were martyrs. The martyrs witness to hope in the Resurrection in the most radical way possible, by counting their lives as nothing for the sake of Christ, who will raise them and vindicate them. Even before the phenomenon of Christian martyrdom, the link between resurrection and willingness to die for God is expressed by the Maccabean martyrs (an Old Testament story that was very influential for Christians in understanding their own heroic deaths). The mother of the seven martyred brothers encourages her sons, putting her faith into these words:

> I do not know how you came into being in my womb. It was not I who gave you life and breath, nor I who set in order the elements within each of you. Therefore the Creator of the world, who shaped the beginning of humankind and devised the origin of all things, will in his mercy give life and breath back to you again, since you now forget yourselves for the sake of his laws. (2 Mc 7:22–23)

For a Christian example of this attitude, we can look to the martyr Apollonius (d. 185). Like the Maccabees, he confesses that he is willing to die because he has been taught "to worship the immortal God, to believe that the soul is immortal, to be convinced that there will be a judgment after death, and that there will be a reward given by God after the resurrection" (*The Martyrdom of Apollonius*, trans. Herbert Musurillo).

In short, then, a saint's body is an object of veneration because it will be raised on the last day and enter into glory. Because Christians believe that they will one day be reunited to their bodies, they believe that the body of the saint is in a very real way that same holy person to whom they might pray or about whom they might read. By venerating a saint's body, we are venerating something that will enter into eternal life. To think of it from another angle, we treat the body of a saint as we would treat the body of someone living whom we respect and love. We honor it, we might even kiss it. In *Martyrdom of Polycarp*, the saint is treated in just this manner by his flock even before his death. The author of the account tells us that the faithful were accustomed to untie Polycarp's sandals, since they "always vied with each other to see which of them would be the first to touch his body. Even before his martyrdom, he had always been honored for holiness of life" (*Martyrdom of Polycarp* 13.2, trans. James A. Kleist).

Catholic veneration of saints' bodies, then, is a concrete act of faith in the resurrection of the body, just as our prayers for the intercession of the saints are concrete acts of faith in the everlasting life of heaven. The practice of the veneration of relics is also a strong endorsement of the doctrine of creation. The Christian understanding of creation is that God created all things from nothing and that creation is good (see the repeated use of this word in Genesis 1). This truth is not at all obvious. Many might look around at the world today and decide it is not very good, and they might look at their own bodies that can be weak and ill and wish to escape from them. Even some early Christian groups denied that God the Father of Jesus Christ was also the creator of the world, such as the Christians known as the "gnostics." Gnostics saw much evil in the world, and they attributed that evil to our bodies. After all, our bodies seem often to be the source of our temptations. They get hungry and tired, and even more than that, often they want to eat and sleep more than they ought!

Paul gives us a very different picture of the body, however. He asks the Corinthians indignantly: "Or do you not know that your body is a temple of the Holy Spirit within you, which you have from God, and that you are not your own? For you were bought with a price; therefore glorify God in your body" (1 Cor 6:19–20). Paul is exhorting the Corinthians to live morally, especially in matters that pertain to the body (in this case, he is concerned with sexual morality). His reasoning is along these lines: Christ himself took a body and sacrificed it for our salvation so that now our bodies may be dwelling places of the Holy Spirit. Let us treat our bodies accordingly.

The Christian view is that we *are* our bodies; that is, we are both body and soul. Our true identity is not found apart from the body. We consume God in the Eucharist with our bodies, we worship God with our bodies, we do good works in our bodies. So when we venerate the bodies of the saints, we reaffirm this fundamental reality about what we are as human beings and what we are created for. We also affirm that the world is good and that people can live a good life in it.

The veneration of relics is an ancient part of the Church's worship, therefore, and for sound theological reasons (i.e., our belief in the goodness of the body and its resurrection on the last day). Nevertheless, one cannot deny that there have been many abuses pertaining to relics. Relics have been stolen, bought and sold, and treated like magical objects. Such practices one would not call respectful, nor do they fall under the heading of "veneration." If nothing else, however, this zeal (or this exploitation of others' zeal) for relics can tell us something of their power. Because of these abuses, in the year 1215 the Fourth Lateran Council decreed that all relics should be displayed in a case, to prevent their surreptitious sale or improper use. This council was not the first to make decrees surrounding the proper use of relics, but it helps explain the near universal practice today of keeping relics in reliquaries (special boxes or cases).

Catholic veneration of relics, moreover, goes beyond the respectful honoring of the body of some holy person. The Church also allows the bodies of canonized saints to be divided and distributed among churches. Given that the earliest relics were bones (as in the case of Polycarp), we can see that such sharing would be easily achieved. Although some of these practices might at first be unsettling to us, it is logical that as the cults of the saints grew, all the faithful wanted access to relics, and this can only be made possible by sharing them. The idea that a saint's relics could be transferred and shared, even if it meant dividing up the body, is also very ancient. Already by the time of Augustine in the fourth century, the faithful were dividing the relics of the saints amongst their churches. Augustine's own church received some relics of St. Stephen, and he recounts many miracles being worked through them. This made Augustine much more interested in the miraculous later in life than he had been earlier on.

Perhaps we can see in this practice another indication of the special role that the canonized saints play in the worship of God, which is precisely what their status as "canonized" qualifies them for, as discussed in chapter 10. The spreading of relics throughout the churches means that the saints are tangibly and universally incorporated into the Church's life. In the Western Church, every altar has a relic either underneath it or inside the altar stone; in the East, it is sewn inside the altar cloth. Canonized saints have therefore been incorporated into the Mass in a unique way, by their near ubiquitous true presence on the altars of the Church.

13. WHAT DOES IT MEAN TO TAKE A SAINT'S NAME AT CONFIRMATION OR TO BE NAMED AFTER A SAINT?

Naming has always been very important in human culture, and there is plenty of evidence of this in the Bible. We are told in Genesis 2 that the animals are brought to Adam so that he can name them (v. 19). The names of many figures in the Old Testament have special meaning—God changes the name of Abram to Abraham and Sarai to Sarah after he makes a covenant with them (see Genesis 17:1–15). This momentous occasion is recalled in the book of Nehemiah: "You are the LORD, the God who chose Abram and brought him out of Ur of the Chaldeans and gave him the name Abraham" (9:7). Sarah, in turn, names the son of her old age Isaac, which means "laughter," because although Sarah had laughed at God when he promised her a son, God nevertheless brought the joy of laughter to her through that son (Gn 21:6). Jacob's name is changed to Israel, which means "the one who strives with God," after he wrestles with an angel, and this name becomes that of a whole nation (Gn 32:28). In the New Testament, the angel Gabriel tells Zechariah to give the name John to his son (Lk 1:13) and tells Mary that her son's name should be Jesus (Lk 1:31). Jesus himself renames Simon and calls him Peter, saying, "Blessed are you, Simon son of Jonah! For flesh and blood has not revealed this to you, but my Father in heaven. And I tell you, you are Peter, and on this rock I will build my church, and the gates of Hades will not prevail against it" (Mt 16:17–18).

The idea that a name signals something important about a person's identity or destiny is captured in a Latin idiom: *nomen est omen*, meaning "a name is an omen." A similar idea is evident when the New Testament speaks of Christians having their names written in the book of life, affirming their heavenly destiny (see Philippians 4:3; Revelation 13:8, 20:12, 21:27). The ancients believed that knowing someone's true name could give you power over them, as is evidenced even in much later folktales such as that of Rumpelstiltskin. Christians have the name of Christ written upon their foreheads (Rv 14:1, 22:4, alluding to the baptismal seal of the Cross), which indicates their true identity, and Revelation also tells us that Christ will give "a new name . . . which no one knows except him who receives it" (Rv 2:17). The idea behind these passages is that Christians belong to Christ alone, and in the Last Judgment he and no other will have power and authority over them. When all is at last revealed, there will be no spiritual identity theft.

All of these biblical passages and ancient beliefs play into Christian naming practices. To be clear, there has never been a universal practice of getting a special name at Baptism (or at Confirmation) or of naming children after saints. Early Christians continued to name children after their family members. They also sometimes picked names that were Christian but not specifically the name of a saint—such as the name of a virtue (a contemporary example is Charity) or a feast day (an example is Noelle). Nevertheless, some version of taking the names of the saints has been around since the earliest days of Christianity. Some Christians added a saint's name to their own out of devotion—perhaps at their (adult) baptism. One such example is church historian Eusebius of Caesarea, who went by Eusebius Pamphili because of his love of the martyr Pamphilus. Dionysius of Alexandria in the third century refers to the pious practice of naming children after Sts. John, Peter, and Paul (see Eusebius, *Ecclesiastical History* 7.25.14). John Chrysostom in the fourth century mentions people naming their children after the martyr Meletius (*On Saint Meletius* 2) and chastises his flock for following superstitious pagan naming practices rather than picking the names of the saints for their children (see *Homily* 12 *on 1*

Cor); the practice he is criticizing apparently involved family members holding a candle, and the one whose candle burned the longest had the child named after him. Melania the Elder (see Rufinus's *Apology* 2.26) and Macrina the Younger (see *Life of Macrina* 2) were even said to have a "secret name" or alternate name, perhaps like the one mentioned in Revelation. In the cases of both women that name was Thecla, referring back to a well-known early Christian martyr.

Since naming a child usually happens shortly after birth, it was natural to bestow a name on a child at the time of baptism once infant baptism became the universal practice of the Church. Later a person's first name became known as their "Christian name," that is, the name with which they were presented at their christening. Today, canon law allows a child to be given any name at baptism so long as it is not explicitly against the Christian faith (for example, giving the child the name of a demon or a pagan god). A person's first name, then, came to be called a "Christian name" whether it was the name of a saint or not.

Nevertheless, it continued to be a common practice of the faithful to give their children the names of saints, and various rules have been enforced to that effect at different times and in different places. Sometimes the name of the child was chosen based on the feast day on which they were baptized—to take a famous example, Martin Luther (born in 1483) was given his name after St. Martin of Tours, since Luther was baptized on Martin's feast day (November 8). Later on, when the Confirmation of a child took place at an older age (originally, Confirmation and Baptism occurred at the same time in infancy), this also became a natural time to pick a saint to be a patron. Sometimes the name chosen would correspond to the given Christian name and sometimes not, but in the case of a Confirmation name, the practice bears more resemblance to that of Eusebius (taking a saint's name out of devotion) or Macrina and Melania (having a secret or alternate name), because the saint's name chosen at Confirmation is rarely a name by which the confirmandi is actually known or called. On the whole, then, naming children after a saint or taking a saint's name for yourself is best understood as a pious practice with a venerable tradition, but it is not something universal or required by the Church.

What is the meaning of these practices? If naming is powerful, then following after a saint and taking their life as a kind of omen for your own life can be equally powerful. If you are naming a child, the name offers the child a model and expresses your desire for their sanctity. If you are choosing a name in Confirmation, the name expresses the model that you desire for yourself. Perhaps the clearest example of the fruit of this devotion comes from the lives of saints who—taking the names of other saints and imitating them—have themselves joined the rank of canonized saints along with their patrons.

Frances Xavier Cabrini is an incredible and multilayered example. Let's start with the first saint in this name chain.

Francis of Assisi (1181–1226) is a well-known Catholic saint. Francis helped to renew the Church by his radical life of poverty and conformity to Christ. Others followed him, and he became the founder of the Franciscan order. He is known for his simplicity of life and his love of the poor and of all God's creation. He was also the first saint to receive the stigmata—the wounds of Christ, a visible sign of his likeness to the poor Crucified One. Francis, however, was born to a wealthy family, and his father was a cloth merchant. As a young man he lived a carefree life, dressing in fine clothes and spending time with his wealthy friends. And so we can see that another great saint, given the name Francis by his parents, followed in many ways after his patron. Francis Xavier (1506–1552) was Spanish but was also born into a wealthy and influential family and was reluctant to become a priest. However, he was persuaded by Ignatius of Loyola to live his life for Christ, and he became one of the original founders of the Jesuits. He then became a famous missionary, working with his Jesuit brothers throughout Southeast Asia to win souls for Christ.

Then we come to St. Frances Xavier Cabrini (1850–1917), who took Francis Xavier as her patron when she entered religious life. Like the two Francises before her, she is the founder of a religious community, called the Missionary Sisters of the Sacred Heart of Jesus. Although she had originally wanted to go to China like the first Francis Xavier, Frances Cabrini's mission was not to the East but to the West, helping poor Italian immigrants to the United States. In a way, then, she combines the charisms of both her namesakes, because she was a missionary far from home like Francis Xavier, but she cared for the Italian poor like Francis of Assisi. Cabrini was the first American citizen to be canonized.

There are many other saints who bear the name Francis as well, such as two saints who were close friends: Francis de Sales (1567–1622) and Jane Frances de Chantal (1572–1641). Francis de Sales was Jane Frances's spiritual director, and he wrote the classic *Introduction to the Devout Life* for her. We can think of many more saint lineages, such as three great Teresas: Teresa of Avila (ca. 1515–1582), Thérèse of Lisieux (1873–1897), and Teresa of Calcutta (1910–1997). And it would take a long time to count all of the Johns and their relationship to one another, even if we looked no further than the Bible and the early church! It is amazing to see what God has worked through his saints and how he allows us to be united to one another in so many ways, including in this special devotion of taking the names of the saints for our own. Just as we can name children after family members out of love or respect, so also we can name our children after those in our heavenly family and who are one with us, the saints. If the old Latin saying is true, that a name helps define our destiny, being able to take and give such noble names is truly a blessing. And if we were ever in doubt that the saints are companions in this life as we make our way to heaven, we can look to our namesakes and to our Confirmation patrons.

14.

WHY DO SAINTS HAVE FEAST DAYS, WHAT DO THEY MEAN, AND HOW CAN I CELEBRATE THEM?

As we have already read, the companions of St. Polycarp who collected his bones also returned to the resting place of those relics on what they termed his "birthday," which was the day of Polycarp's death. This day was understood to be his true birthday (his *dies natalis*, as it would become known in Latin) because on that day he entered eternal life. The memorials of the saints have traditionally followed this pattern, namely, that the saint is honored on the day of his or her death; thus the whole calendar year became dotted with these special celebrations in honor of the saints. The word "holiday" in fact comes from "holy day" and was a generic term for a special religious day. Advent is then fittingly referred to as "the holidays" (i.e., the holy days) since so many popular feast days (such as the Feasts of St. Nicholas, the Immaculate Conception, St. Lucy, and Our Lady of Guadalupe) are celebrated during the season, although of course today the term "holiday" has taken on a much broader meaning, encompassing a variety of celebrations and vacations.

Over the centuries and millennia, however, the Church has been blessed with so many canonized saints that there are not enough days in the year to formally celebrate each and every one of them. The Church has arranged the modern Roman calendar to require the veneration of major saints and to keep Lent free of too many feast days in order that the fasting season may be clearly set apart and kept more easily. Because of these various concerns, often a saint's feast day is changed from their death day to some other day (sometimes to a day close to their death day or to some other significant day for that saint). And although the terms "holy day" and "feast day" are normally used very generally, the modern Roman calendar divides holy days into three technical categories: solemnities, feasts, and memorials.

Solemnities are the most important holy days of the Church and celebrate the chief mysteries of the faith—such as Christmas, Easter, and Pentecost—or honor the foremost among the saints who played an important role in salvation history, such as the Virgin Mary, Joseph, and John the Baptist. In terms of the liturgy, you might notice that on these days (even if they are weekdays) the Gloria is sung and there is an extra reading, and there may also be special prayers or changes to prayers to honor the day. The bishops in a certain region can decide to declare a solemnity a holy day of obligation, meaning that the faithful are required to go to Mass on that day. Indeed, the calendar varies from region to region with respect to how certain solemnities are kept. For example, the Ascension of Our Lord and Corpus Christi are in some places observed on Thursday and in others on the closest Sunday.

A feast (in the technical sense, that is) is next in order of importance and marks a significant event in the life of Christ (such as his baptism or the Presentation in the Temple) or of other important saints, such as the apostles and archangels. On feasts the Gloria is also sung, and special readings are chosen for that day. Lastly are memorials, which honor many other canonized saints (or more minor events and devotions of Christ or Mary). There can be special readings and prayers used for these days. Some memorials must be kept (called obligatory memorials), but others are optional, so a particular priest can decide whether or not to honor a particular saint on that day. For certain groups (for example, a parish named after a saint or a religious community founded by a particular saint), the status of certain holy days might be elevated. We also celebrate the special solemnity of All Saints' Day on November 1 to make sure that none of the saints are left out of the calendar, whether known or unknown. On All Saints' Day you might hear a litany of the saints sung in the liturgy, asking for the intercession of many different canonized saints in a long list. These distinctions and calendrical arrangements are made (carefully and painstakingly) to help both the clergy and the faithful keep track of holy days more easily, since the list of feasts and of saints is quite long! Nevertheless, despite the intentional arrangement, it can take a lifetime to fully understand, remember, and note the various days.

In addition to the Church's official calendar, there are also many canonized saints whose feast days are not formally listed as an optional memorial in the liturgy. They can still be remembered in private devotions on their feast day, their intercession can be sought in prayer, or their relics can be honored especially on that day.

There is no question that the Church's calendar can be confusing, even when described in the simplest terms possible as we have just done, but that should come as no surprise. The calendar, after all, is one of the most important and complex things in our everyday life—perhaps in modernity more so than ever. In ages past, the Church's calendar allowed the rhythm of life to be sacred, to remind us that we are passing through time but headed toward eternity. The same seasons and feasts come round and round again as a moving image of that eternity. Being in tune with the Church's calendar helps us to see history not simply as one thing after another, but as the unfolding of God's harmonious plan. The feasts are a kind of baseline in the structure of our lives, a solid, holy ground upon which to found our day-to-day activities. The Church's calendar is also another reminder of the three-dimensional nature of her communion that we have mentioned before—the communion of God and humankind and of all of us with one another, across time and space. The feasts we celebrate today were celebrated by the very saints who are incorporated into the liturgy and put us in communion with them.

Living our lives by the Church's calendar might sound appealing, but we do not live in medieval Europe where the world runs according to Christian feasts. We have a multitude of competing calendar dates—the school year, the calendar year, the fiscal year, and so on. How can we make some progress toward keeping these holy days and allowing the rhythm of the Church's life to help ground and shape our fast-paced schedule? How can we make the saints a part of our day-to-day planning?

There are, of course, many different ways of keeping these feasts. If you want to be more intentional about remembering saints' feasts, the easiest first step would be to buy a Catholic calendar that lists the feast days on it. Or, if you want to avoid getting overwhelmed by seeing every single feast day, you could look up the feast days of a few saints special to you and your family and mark those days on your calendar (whatever kind you use). The simplest way to observe their feast day is to pray to them and ask for their intercession on that day. Of course, the most traditional and significant way to mark the feast is to go to Mass. This is how Monica, mother of Augustine, asked to be remembered after her death (although she was, of course, not thinking of herself as a canonized saint at the time but as a soul in need of prayers). Augustine tells us of her request shortly before her death:

> On the day when her release was at hand she gave no thought to costly burial or the embalming of her body with spices, nor did she pine for a special monument or concern herself about a grave in her native land; no, that was not her command to us. She desired only to be remembered at your altar, where she had served you with never a day's absence. (*Confessions* 9.13.36, trans. Maria Boulding)

It is in the Eucharist where we are most intimately united to the saints, it is in the altar that the saint's relics are present, and it is at the Mass that we join the saints in their heavenly occupation—all ideas that we have encountered already. And so also the Mass is the most fitting "birthday party" of the saints, where we can come into their presence and celebrate with them. If it is not possible to go to Mass, you could pray with the Office of Readings, which sometimes includes writings of a saint on their feast day and prayers appropriate to the day.

Then, of course, there many traditional devotions on a particular saint's feast day that can be fun to follow and can help make the day memorable. On St. Nicholas's Day, it is traditional to leave presents in people's shoes (usually chocolate and an orange). On St. Lucy's Day, candles are especially appropriate (for her name means "light"). On St. Blaise's Day, churches often offer a blessing of the throat (Blaise is the patron of throat ailments, as he was said to have saved a choking child). St. Patrick's Day is celebrated extravagantly by the Irish (and anyone who wants to be Irish for a day). Many people pray an Advent novena starting on St. Andrew's Day. There are many such traditions—you can find books with recipes or traditions for particular feasts, and many other ideas or cultural practices online. Following any of these recommendations, of course, is by no means necessary to celebrate appropriately, and some may come more naturally than others, depending on where you live and the existing traditions of your own family. And like a party for any earthly friend, your celebration does not have to be overly complicated; it usually involves good cheer and probably some good food.

CONCLUSION

May the angels lead you into paradise;
may the martyrs receive you at your arrival
and lead you to the holy city Jerusalem.
May choirs of angels receive you
and with Lazarus, once a poor man,
may you have eternal rest.

As we began with a prayer from the Mass, let us end by recalling this prayer from the requiem Mass. The angels and saints are our companions in this sojourn on earth. They guard us, they intercede for us, they worship with us, they are united with us in the Body of Christ. God has multiplied his saints, and the treasure of their relics fills our churches. Even the days of the year are marked with the names of the saints, by the memory of their happy death; "precious in the sight of the LORD is the death of his faithful ones" (Ps 116:15).

But to what end is this friendship of ours with the angels and saints? To what end is learning more about them and about the practices of the Church dedicated to them? To what end is attending the Mass with more understanding and practicing our devotions to saints and angels more fervently?

To the end expressed in the above prayer: that we too may die in friendship with God and his saints, so that at the end of our earthly life, the angels and saints whom we have come to know, and all those who have died in the peace of Christ, may come out to meet us, "with shouts of joy, carrying their sheaves" (Ps 126:6). We celebrate with the Church in this life so that in the next the Church triumphant may eagerly await our arrival at the gates of the heavenly Jerusalem, that they may recognize us because we are part of their fellowship. After all, the saints and angels do not desire our friendship for their own sake, as if they would be greater heroes for earning fame on earth. Rather, the saints and angels desire our friendship because they are friends of Christ. They desire that their fame invite us to imitation; they love us as brothers and sisters in Christ. We are not in competition with the merits of the saints, for they wish even for their good deeds to be counted together with ours. They cry with us in the Mass, "Look not on our sins but on the faith of your Church."

Hopefully this book has been an occasion for you to marvel at the great gift God has given to his Church in putting his holy angels in fellowship with us and at our service, and by giving us so many holy saints whom we might take as patrons here on earth and be with forever in heaven. Hopefully you have come to see that in the communion of saints the deepest desire of the human heart is met—that we might know and love God perfectly and that we might know and love each other perfectly. Christ has accomplished the perfect union of God and man and of all of humanity (and of all rational creatures) in himself, while also empowering and enlivening all our human efforts to that end, we who are incorporated into his body. In thinking about the angelic life and in contemplating the human lives of the saints, we can marvel at God's abundant mercy in issuing forth so many holy ones and in bringing all of them to perfection in himself and to life everlasting.

Elizabeth Klein is an assistant professor of theology at the Augustine Institute, a contributor to Formed, and the author of *God: What Every Catholic Should Know* and *Augustine's Theology of Angels*.

She is the director of the Augustine Institute's Short Course Program. Klein earned a doctor of philosophy degree in historical theology at the University of Notre Dame, where she also served as a post-doctoral scholar, course instructor, and graduate assistant. She earned bachelor's and master's degrees from McMaster University.

Klein is a regular contributor to *Magnificat*. She has been a guest on a number of radio shows and podcasts, including *Church Life Journal Radio*, *Classical Theism*, and *The Catholic Gentleman*. She has spoken at the Denver Catholic Women's Conference, Fullness of Truth, and the Augustine Institute Bible Conference.

She lives with her family in Aurora, Colorado.

https://www.augustineinstitute.org/faculty-and-staff/elizabeth-klein-ph-d
Formed.org

The McGrath Institute for Church Life was founded as the Center for Pastoral and Social Ministry by the late Notre Dame President Fr. Theodore Hesburgh, C.S.C., in 1976. The McGrath Institute partners with Catholic dioceses, parishes, and schools to provide theological education and formation to address pressing pastoral problems. The Institute connects the Catholic intellectual life to the life of the Church to form faithful Catholic leaders for service to the Church and the world. The McGrath Institute strives to be the preeminent source of creative Catholic content and programming for the new evangelization.

Brant Pitre is a Catholic theologian and bestselling author.

MORE IN THE **ENGAGING CATHOLICISM SERIES**

Books in the Engaging Catholicism series from the McGrath Institute for Church Life at the University of Notre Dame help readers discover the beauty and truth of the Catholic faith through a concise exploration of the Church's most important but often difficult-to-grasp doctrines as well as crucial pastoral and spiritual practices. Perfect for seekers and new Catholics, clergy and catechetical leaders, and everyone in between, the series expands the McGrath Institute's mission to connect the Catholic intellectual life at Notre Dame to the pastoral life of the Church and the spiritual needs of her people.

Look for these titles wherever books and eBooks are sold.
Visit **avemariapress.com** to learn more.